Reading and Note Taking Study Guide

AMERICAN
HISTORY

PEARSON

Boston, Massachusetts • Chandler, Arizona • Glenview, Illinois • New York, New York

Acknowledgments

Grateful acknowledgment is made to the following for copyrighted material:

Images:
Cover: Chris Cheadle/Alamy

13-digit ISBN:	978-0-32-888041-6
10-digit ISBN:	0-32-888041-8
6 7 8 9 10	19 18 17

Contents

American History
Reading and Note Taking Study Guide

How to Use the *Reading and Note Taking Study Guide*

The **Reading and Note Taking Study Guide** will help you better understand the content of *American History*. This section will also develop your reading, vocabulary, and note taking skills. Each study guide consists of three components. The first component focuses on developing graphic organizers that will help you take notes as you read.

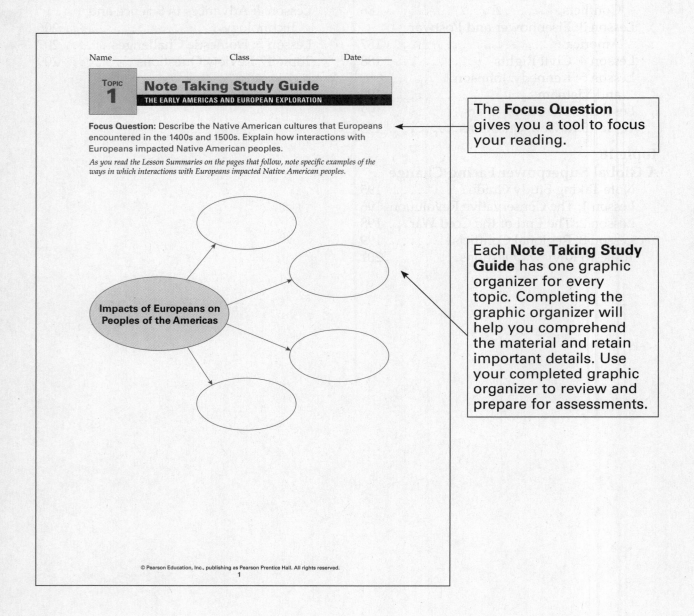

Name_____ Class_____ Date_____

TOPIC
1

Note Taking Study Guide
THE EARLY AMERICAS AND EUROPEAN EXPLORATION

Focus Question: Describe the Native American cultures that Europeans encountered in the 1400s and 1500s. Explain how interactions with Europeans impacted Native American peoples.

As you read the Lesson Summaries on the pages that follow, note specific examples of the ways in which interactions with Europeans impacted Native American peoples.

Impacts of Europeans on Peoples of the Americas

1

The **Focus Question** gives you a tool to focus your reading.

Each **Note Taking Study Guide** has one graphic organizer for every topic. Completing the graphic organizer will help you comprehend the material and retain important details. Use your completed graphic organizer to review and prepare for assessments.

The second component highlights the central themes, issues, and concepts of each section.

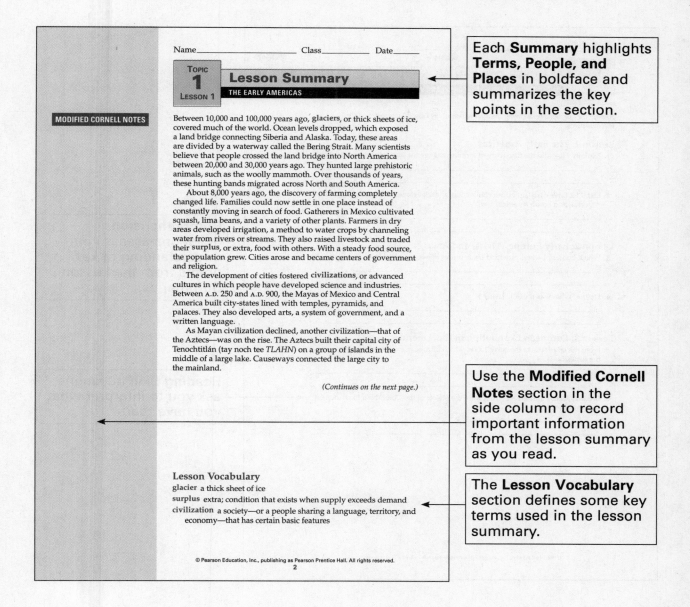

Name_____ Class_____ Date_____

TOPIC
1
LESSON 1

Lesson Summary

THE EARLY AMERICAS

MODIFIED CORNELL NOTES

Between 10,000 and 100,000 years ago, **glaciers**, or thick sheets of ice, covered much of the world. Ocean levels dropped, which exposed a land bridge connecting Siberia and Alaska. Today, these areas are divided by a waterway called the Bering Strait. Many scientists believe that people crossed the land bridge into North America between 20,000 and 30,000 years ago. They hunted large prehistoric animals, such as the woolly mammoth. Over thousands of years, these hunting bands migrated across North and South America.

About 8,000 years ago, the discovery of farming completely changed life. Families could now settle in one place instead of constantly moving in search of food. Gatherers in Mexico cultivated squash, lima beans, and a variety of other plants. Farmers in dry areas developed irrigation, a method to water crops by channeling water from rivers or streams. They also raised livestock and traded their **surplus**, or extra, food with others. With a steady food source, the population grew. Cities arose and became centers of government and religion.

The development of cities fostered **civilizations**, or advanced cultures in which people have developed science and industries. Between A.D. 250 and A.D. 900, the Mayas of Mexico and Central America built city-states lined with temples, pyramids, and palaces. They also developed arts, a system of government, and a written language.

As Mayan civilization declined, another civilization—that of the Aztecs—was on the rise. The Aztecs built their capital city of Tenochtitlán (tay noch tee *TLAHN*) on a group of islands in the middle of a large lake. Causeways connected the large city to the mainland.

(Continues on the next page.)

Lesson Vocabulary
glacier a thick sheet of ice
surplus extra; condition that exists when supply exceeds demand
civilization a society—or a people sharing a language, territory, and
    economy—that has certain basic features

2

Each **Summary** highlights **Terms, People, and Places** in boldface and summarizes the key points in the section.

Use the **Modified Cornell Notes** section in the side column to record important information from the lesson summary as you read.

The **Lesson Vocabulary** section defines some key terms used in the lesson summary.

The third component consists of review questions that assess your understanding of the section.

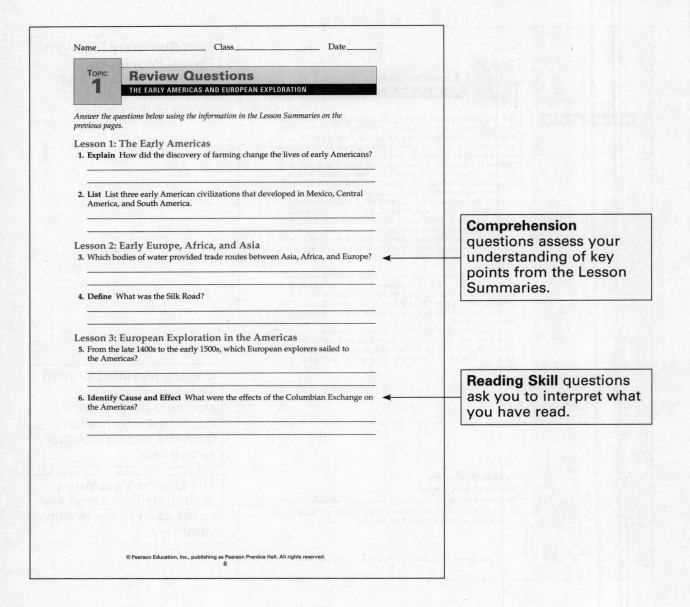

Name_____ Class_____ Date_____

Answer the questions below using the information in the Lesson Summaries on the previous pages.

Lesson 1: The Early Americas

1. **Explain** How did the discovery of farming change the lives of early Americans?
_____
_____

2. **List** List three early American civilizations that developed in Mexico, Central America, and South America.
_____
_____

Lesson 2: Early Europe, Africa, and Asia

3. Which bodies of water provided trade routes between Asia, Africa, and Europe? ◄
_____
_____

4. **Define** What was the Silk Road?
_____
_____

Lesson 3: European Exploration in the Americas

5. From the late 1400s to the early 1500s, which European explorers sailed to the Americas?
_____
_____

6. **Identify Cause and Effect** What were the effects of the Columbian Exchange on ◄ the Americas?
_____
_____

Comprehension questions assess your understanding of key points from the Lesson Summaries.

Reading Skill questions ask you to interpret what you have read.

TOPIC 1

Note Taking Study Guide

THE EARLY AMERICAS AND EUROPEAN EXPLORATION

Focus Question: Describe the Native American cultures that Europeans encountered in the 1400s and 1500s. Explain how interactions with Europeans impacted Native American peoples.

As you read the Lesson Summaries on the pages that follow, note specific examples of the ways in which interactions with Europeans impacted Native American peoples.

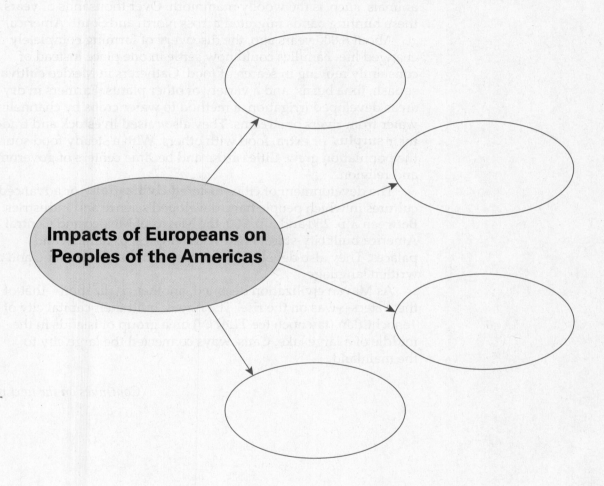

Impacts of Europeans on Peoples of the Americas

TOPIC 1 LESSON 1

Lesson Summary

THE EARLY AMERICAS

Between 10,000 and 100,000 years ago, **glaciers**, or thick sheets of ice, covered much of the world. Ocean levels dropped, which exposed a land bridge connecting Siberia and Alaska. Today, these areas are divided by a waterway called the Bering Strait. Many scientists believe that people crossed the land bridge into North America between 20,000 and 30,000 years ago. They hunted large prehistoric animals, such as the woolly mammoth. Over thousands of years, these hunting bands migrated across North and South America.

About 8,000 years ago, the discovery of farming completely changed life. Families could now settle in one place instead of constantly moving in search of food. Gatherers in Mexico cultivated squash, lima beans, and a variety of other plants. Farmers in dry areas developed irrigation, a method to water crops by channeling water from rivers or streams. They also raised livestock and traded their **surplus**, or extra, food with others. With a steady food source, the population grew. Cities arose and became centers of government and religion.

The development of cities fostered **civilizations**, or advanced cultures in which people have developed science and industries. Between A.D. 250 and A.D. 900, the Mayas of Mexico and Central America built city-states lined with temples, pyramids, and palaces. They also developed arts, a system of government, and a written language.

As Mayan civilization declined, another civilization—that of the Aztecs—was on the rise. The Aztecs built their capital city of Tenochtitlán (tay noch tee *TLAHN*) on a group of islands in the middle of a large lake. Causeways connected the large city to the mainland.

(Continues on the next page.)

Lesson Vocabulary

glacier a thick sheet of ice

surplus extra; condition that exists when supply exceeds demand

civilization a society—or a people sharing a language, territory, and economy—that has certain basic features

TOPIC 1
LESSON 1

Lesson Summary
THE EARLY AMERICAS

(Continued from page 2)

In the 1400s, the Incas built the world's largest empire in South America. Their rule extended along the Andes, across the Atacama Desert, and into the edge of the Amazon rain forest.

People in North America developed unique **cultures**, or ways of life. The Mound Builders began to emerge about 3,000 years ago between the Appalachian Mountains and the Mississippi Valley. They constructed large mounds to use as burial places and as the base for public buildings.

The Anasazi were a very different culture located in southern Utah, Colorado, northern Arizona, and New Mexico. They made baskets, pottery, and jewelry. Their homes were cliff dwellings, which they mysteriously abandoned by 1300.

Scholars organize Native Americans into **culture areas**, or regions in which groups of people have a similar way of life. Many culture areas share some basic traits.

Eastern Woodlands people hunted, fished, and foraged for plants in the heavy forests. Some began farming by A.D. 1000. The Algonquin people dominated southern Canada and the Great Lakes. The Iroquois, in what is now New York, comprised five nations. Each nation had **clans**, or groups of families related to one another. Women owned all clan property and chose the clan's **sachem**, or tribal chief.

Lesson Vocabulary

culture an entire way of life developed by a people

culture area a region in which people share a similar way of life

clan a group of two or more related families

sachem a tribal chief of a Northeastern tribe; a member of the council of chiefs in the League of the Iroquois

TOPIC 1 — LESSON 2

Lesson Summary
EARLY EUROPE, AFRICA, AND ASIA

MODIFIED CORNELL NOTES

Rome fell to invaders in A.D. 476, and Europe fragmented into small states, ushering in the thousand-year-long Middle Ages. By the ninth century, kings and nobles relied on **feudalism**, in which a ruler grants parts of his lands to lords in exchange for military and financial assistance. Daily life revolved around the Catholic Church. In 1095, Pope Urban II declared a **crusade**, or holy war, to win control of the Holy Land from Muslims. Although the Crusades ultimately failed, they did introduce the Europeans to the riches and navigation technology of the advanced Muslim civilization.

By the 1500s, a complex trade network linked Europe, Africa, and Asia, much of it passing through the Arabian Peninsula. Ships from China and India brought spices, silks, and gems to Red Sea ports, where they were taken overland to the Middle East.

Trade helped the rise of Islam. This religion was founded in the Arabian Peninsula in the A.D. 600s by the prophet Muhammad. He taught that there is one true God. Followers of Islam, called Muslims, believed that the Quran, the sacred book of Islam, contained the word of God as revealed to Muhammad. Arab armies spread Islam through conquest to North Africa and Spain. Muslim merchants also introduced the religion far into Africa's interior and to Persia and India, where millions of people converted, or changed from one religion to another.

Arab scholars made important contributions to learning and technology. They helped develop algebra and made other contributions in mathematics, medicine, and astronomy. They improved ship technology by introducing large, triangular sails that caught the wind even if it changed direction.

As early as 3100 B.C., Egyptians established trade routes throughout the eastern Mediterranean Sea and the Red Sea to bring home cedar logs, silver, and horses. They also traded for ivory, spices, copper, and cattle from south of Egypt.

Trade centers developed in East Africa about 1000 B.C. By the 1400s, Zimbabwe had become powerful from its location on the trade route between Africa's east coast and the interior. Traders paid taxes on goods passing through it. Coastal cities, such as Kilwa, prospered from traders exchanging cloth, pottery, and other goods for gold and ivory from Africa's interior. A slave trade also developed between East Africa and Asia across the Indian Ocean.

(Continues on the next page.)

Lesson Vocabulary

feudalism a system of rule by lords who ruled their own lands but owed loyalty and military service to a monarch

crusade holy war

TOPIC 1
LESSON 2
Lesson Summary
EARLY EUROPE, AFRICA, AND ASIA

(Continued from page 4)

Trade was not limited to eastern Africa, however. Desert nomads from the Middle East crossed the Sahara with camel caravans to reach West Africa. Ghana, the first major trade center in West Africa, was **affluent** because of its location between salt mines and gold fields. War and changing trade routes gradually weakened the kingdom. In the 1200s, Ghana was absorbed into the empire of Mali, ruled by Mansa Musa. A Muslim, Mansa Musa turned Mali's great city of Timbuktu into a center of Islamic learning. Mali declined in the 1400s under a series of weak rulers. Timbuktu was captured by the Songhai in 1468. Like Ghana and Mali, Songhai flourished from the salt, gold, and slave trades.

Unified in 221 B.C., China's empire expanded across Asia, linked by highways, canals, and a postal system. As China's borders grew, so did its trade. This was made possible by advances in **navigation**, the science of locating the position and plotting the course of ships, and inventions like the magnetic compass. The compass allowed sailors to lose sight of land and still bring the ship back home.

By the 1300s, Chinese traders used sea routes extending from Japan to East Africa. The Chinese explorer Zheng He visited 30 nations in Asia and Africa with his fleet of giant ships. A famous trade route on land was the Silk Road. It was not really one road but rather a 5,000-mile series of routes stretching from Xian, China, to Persia. Silks, spices, bronze goods, and pottery flowed west from China on this route. Merchants carried these goods across Asia to markets in the Middle East and Europe.

In the 1300s, the Renaissance revived interest in ancient Greece and Rome. Art, science, and inventions flourished. Powerful nation-states arose. Spain, Portugal, France, and England shifted trade routes to the Atlantic Ocean.

In 1517, the German monk Martin Luther demanded that the Catholic Church reform itself. Those who joined him in protesting certain practices of the Church were called Protestants. Over time, the Protestants formed their own churches, which pushed Europe into a series of religious wars.

Prince Henry the Navigator hoped to expand Portuguese power and spread Christianity to new lands. In the 1400s, he set up a navigation center at Sagres, where sailors learned to use maps, the magnetic compass, and the astrolabe. With these skills, Portuguese sailors opened the way for exploration.

Lesson Vocabulary

affluent rich or wealthy

navigation the science of locating the position and plotting the course of ships

TOPIC 1 LESSON 3

Lesson Summary

EUROPEAN EXPLORATION IN THE AMERICAS

The search for a water route to Asia led to the European discovery of two continents and the exchange of resources between the Eastern and the Western Hemispheres.

Before Christopher Columbus, the only European visitors to the Americas were Vikings, a seagoing people from Scandinavia. They explored Newfoundland in 1001. Almost 500 years later, Italian-born Columbus settled in Portugal, Europe's leading seafaring nation. He hoped to undertake a voyage to Asia by sailing west instead of east. Portugal's king would not pay for such a trip, believing it would be too long and costly. So Columbus moved to Spain and asked for support from Queen Isabella and King Ferdinand. Six years later, they finally agreed.

In August 1492, Columbus's mostly Spanish crew of 90 set sail on small ships—the *Nina*, the *Pinta*, and the *Santa Maria*, covering 170 miles a day. On October 12, an island was sighted and Columbus claimed it for Spain. Believing he was in the Asian islands known as the Indies, Columbus called the people he saw Indians. He sailed to the island of Cuba, at first thinking it was Japan, and then to Hispaniola, where he built a settlement. He returned to Spain in January 1493, reporting that the West Indies were rich in gold. The monarchs made him governor of all land he had claimed for Spain. In September 1493, he returned to the West Indies as commander of 17 ships with 1,500 soldiers, settlers, and priests. The Spanish wanted to colonize and rule the West Indies and convert the people to Christianity. Columbus built another settlement and enslaved Indians to dig for gold. In 1498, his third expedition reached South America, which he mistook for the Asian mainland. He tried to prove this on a fourth voyage in 1502. He died in 1506 in Spain, convinced he had reached Asia.

Other explorers tried to find a western water route to Asia. Italian explorer Amerigo Vespucci sailed twice to the new lands and became convinced that they were not part of Asia. His descriptions led a German mapmaker to label the region "the land of Amerigo," later shortened to "America." In 1510, Spanish colonist Vasco Núñez de Balboa explored the Caribbean coast of what is now Panama. He trekked westward and became the first European to see the Pacific Ocean.

(Continues on the next page.)

Lesson Vocabulary

seafaring skilled at sea travel

colonize to claim, settle, and rule a distant area

Lesson Summary
EUROPEAN EXPLORATION IN THE AMERICAS

(Continued from page 6)

In 1519, Portuguese explorer Ferdinand Magellan searched the South American coast for a strait, a narrow passage that connects two large bodies of water, between the Atlantic and Pacific oceans. He finally found what is now the Strait of Magellan and from there sailed into the Pacific. In the Philippine Islands, he and several others were killed. Only one ship and 18 men returned to Spain in 1522, making them the first to circumnavigate, or travel around, the earth.

The next century began the Columbian Exchange, a transfer of people, products, and ideas between the Eastern and Western Hemispheres. Some exchanges were good. Europeans brought to the new lands hogs, cows, horses, and other animals, as well as plants such as oats and wheat. The Americas introduced llamas and turkeys and crops that now account for one third of the world's food supply. Other exchanges had a negative impact, including the introduction of diseases to which Native Americans had no immunity. Smallpox, chickenpox, measles, and other diseases killed thousands of them.

Lesson Vocabulary

strait narrow passage that connects two large bodies of water

circumnavigate to travel all the way around Earth

Name_____ Class_____ Date_____

Answer the questions below using the information in the Lesson Summaries on the previous pages.

Lesson 1: The Early Americas

1. Explain How did the discovery of farming change the lives of early Americans?

_____

_____

2. List List three early American civilizations that developed in Mexico, Central America, and South America.

_____

_____

_____

Lesson 2: Early Europe, Africa, and Asia

3. Which bodies of water provided trade routes between Asia, Africa, and Europe?

_____

_____

4. Define What was the Silk Road?

_____

_____

Lesson 3: European Exploration in the Americas

5. From the late 1400s to the early 1500s, which European explorers sailed to the Americas?

_____

_____

6. Identify Cause and Effect What were the effects of the Columbian Exchange on the Americas?

_____

_____

Name_____ Class_____ Date_____

Focus Question: Describe the relationships among the peoples from many different cultures who interacted in North America from the arrival of the first European explorers and colonists to the mid-1700s.

As you read the Lesson Summaries on the following pages, note the relationships among the people from different cultures who interacted in North America, beginning with the Spanish explorers and colonists.

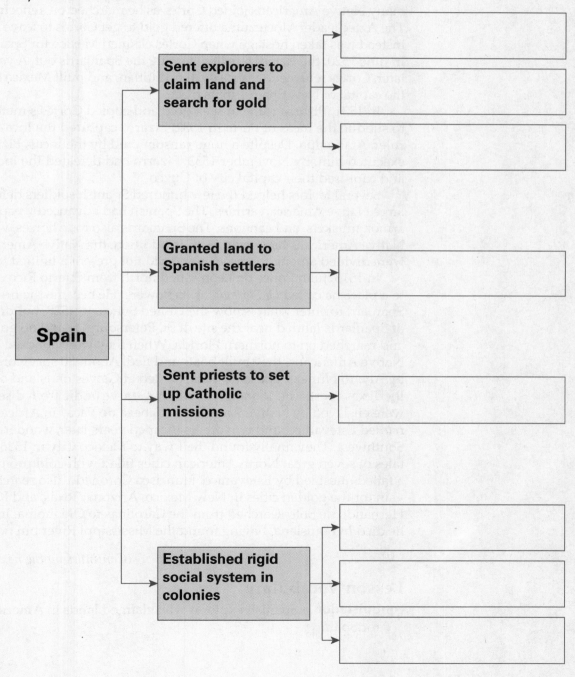

Spain

Sent explorers to claim land and search for gold

Granted land to Spanish settlers

Sent priests to set up Catholic missions

Established rigid social system in colonies

TOPIC 2 LESSON 1

Lesson Summary
SPANISH COLONIZATION AND NEW SPAIN

MODIFIED CORNELL NOTES

The conquests of Hernán Cortés and Francisco Pizarro helped establish a Spanish empire in the Americas. Spanish explorers believed that North America had cities of gold.

Spanish soldier-adventurers called **conquistadors** set out to explore and conquer the new lands. In 1519, Cortés sailed from Cuba to Mexico with more than 500 soldiers, where they were greeted with gifts by Native Americans. Conquered earlier by the brutal Aztecs, many Native Americans joined Cortés as he marched on Tenochtitlán. The Aztec leader Moctezuma offered gold to get Cortés to leave but instead was taken hostage when Cortés claimed Mexico for Spain. In June 1520, the Aztecs rebelled, forcing the Spaniards out. A year later, Cortés returned, destroyed Tenochtitlán, and built Mexico City—the capital of New Spain—in its place.

In 1531, Pizarro came to seek gold and copied Cortés's methods to subdue the Incas of Peru. In 1532, Pizarro captured the Inca ruler, Atahualpa. Despite a huge ransom paid by the Incas, Pizarro executed him. By November 1533, Pizarro had defeated the Incas and captured their capital city of Cuzco.

Several factors helped the few hundred Spanish soldiers defeat large Native American armies. The Spanish had advanced weapons of armor, muskets, and cannons. The Spaniards also rode horses, which Native Americans had never seen. In addition, the Native Americans were divided among themselves and did not present a unified force.

In 1513, Juan Ponce de León sailed north from Puerto Rico to a place he called *La Florida*, for its flowers. He became the first Spaniard to enter what is now the United States. In 1528, hundreds of Spaniards landed near the site of St. Petersburg, found no gold, and marched on to northern Florida. When they were attacked by Native Americans, they built boats and fled. About 80 survivors, led by Álvaro Núñez Cabeza de Vaca, landed at Galveston Island on the Texas coast. The 15 men who did not starve or die from disease were enslaved by Native Americans. Cabeza de Vaca, an African named Estevanico, and two others escaped years later, wandering the Southwest. They finally found their way to Mexico City in 1536. Their tales of seven great North American cities filled with gold prompted a failed quest led by Estevanico. Francisco Coronado also searched in vain for the golden cities in New Mexico, Arizona, Texas, and Kansas. Hernando de Soto searched from the Carolinas to Oklahoma. In 1542, he died in Louisiana, having found the Mississippi River but no gold.

(Continues on the next page.)

Lesson Vocabulary

conquistador a Spanish explorer who claimed lands in America for Spain

MODIFIED CORNELL NOTES

(Continued from page 10)

At first, Spain let the conquistadors administer the lands they had conquered. Later, however, Spain set up a formal system to rule its new colonies. Government officials gave land to settlers to establish mines, ranches, and **plantations**, or large farms. Land grants called *encomiendas* let settlers demand labor or taxes from Native Americans. Forced to work on plantations and in gold and silver mines, many Native Americans died.

A Spanish priest, Bartolomé de Las Casas tried to reform the *encomienda* system. The Spanish set up Catholic **missions**, or religious settlements, to convert Native Americans to Christianity. As the Native American death toll rose, Spanish colonists looked to Africa for new laborers. By the mid-1500s, some 2,000 enslaved Africans were shipped each year to Hispaniola alone.

A rigid social system based on birthplace and blood was established in the Spanish colonies. At the top were *peninsulares*, or colonists born in Spain, which included most government officials. Colonists born in America to Spanish parents were *Creoles* and included wealthy merchants and plantation owners. People of mixed Spanish and Indian parentage, *mestizos*, could do well economically but could never enter the upper levels of society. *Mulattos*, people of Spanish and African heritage, were held at the bottom of society. This class system helped Spain control its American empire for 300 years.

Lesson Vocabulary

plantation a large estate farmed by many workers

encomienda an area of land granted to a Spanish settler with the legal permission to demand labor or taxes from Native Americans

mission a settlement run by Catholic priests and friars whose goal was to convert Indians to Christianity

peninsular a person from Spain who held a position of power in a Spanish colony

TOPIC 2 LESSON 2

Lesson Summary
THE FIRST FRENCH, DUTCH, AND ENGLISH COLONIES

MODIFIED CORNELL NOTES

As the Protestant Reformation spread, the magnitude of the split between Catholics and Protestants became so great that it heightened tensions among European countries.

Wars were common. European rulers no longer trusted one another or their trade alliances.

England, France, and Holland all agreed to pay for voyages to North America to find a **northwest passage**, a sea route from the Atlantic to the Pacific that passed through or around North America.

English explorer Henry Hudson lost support from the English after two failed voyages in the Arctic Ocean in 1607 and 1608. The Dutch supported a third voyage in 1609, which led him to New York and the river later named after him.

By the early 1600s, England, France, and the Netherlands had supported explorations of North America. In 1603, Samuel de Champlain mapped the St. Lawrence River area. Champlain set up the colony's first settlement, a trading post, in Nova Scotia in 1604. Independent traders called *coureurs de bois*, French for "runners of the woods," lived among the Native Americans and went deep into the wilderness to trade for pelts. In 1608, Champlain established Quebec on the banks of the St. Lawrence.

Dutch land claims were based on Henry Hudson's exploration. In 1610, Dutch traders arrived in the Hudson River valley. Their trade with Native Americans was so good that the Dutch West India Company set up a permanent colony, called New Netherland.

Because of the rich profits made from furs, the French and Dutch valued Native Americans as trading partners. In exchange for pelts, the traders provided goods such as cloth, iron pots and tools, and guns. In addition, the French and Dutch made **alliances**, or agreements, with Indian nations. Many alliances, however, proved detrimental to Native Americans and led to warfare among the tribes.

(Continues on the next page.)

Lesson Vocabulary

northwest passage a waterway through or around North America

coureurs de bois a French colonist who lived in the lands beyond French settlements as a fur trapper

alliance an agreement between nations to aid and protect one another

TOPIC 2 LESSON 2 — Lesson Summary
THE FIRST FRENCH, DUTCH, AND ENGLISH COLONIES

(Continued from page 12)

In 1607, a wealthy group formed the Virginia Company of London, hoping their American colony would yield valuable resources. King James I gave the company a **charter**, or document that grants rights, to settle much of the Atlantic coast. In 1607, colonists sailed into Chesapeake Bay and built Jamestown, England's first permanent settlement in North America.

In 1619, colonists were elected to and met in Virginia's legislature—the House of Burgesses. Burgesses could pass laws and set taxes, but they shared power with Virginia's governor. This marked the start of **representative government** in North America, or government in which voters elect people to make laws for them. Also in 1619, a Dutch ship carried captive Africans to Virginia. Some slaves earned their freedom. Permanent slavery did not begin in Virginia until the late 1600s.

Lesson Vocabulary

charter a legal document giving certain rights to a person or company

representative government a political system in which voters elect representatives to make laws for them

TOPIC 2 LESSON 3

Lesson Summary
THE NEW ENGLAND COLONIES

MODIFIED CORNELL NOTES

In the 1500s, people wishing to separate from the Church of England were **persecuted**, or treated unfairly because of their religious beliefs. Some Separatists settled in Holland to practice Christianity in their own way. Still unhappy, one group left for Virginia in 1620. Today, we call these people the Pilgrims. A **pilgrim** is a person who takes a religious journey. In September 1620, they sailed for Virginia on the *Mayflower*, but storms along the way drove them north to Plymouth, Massachusetts. Before going ashore, 41 men signed the Mayflower Compact, the first document in which colonists claimed self-government. Half the colonists died that winter from hunger or disease. A Native American, Squanto, showed them how to plant corn, beans, and pumpkins. In 1621, the Pilgrims gave thanks, which is celebrated today as Thanksgiving.

The Puritans, a group larger than the Pilgrims, wanted to reform, not separate from, the Church of England. They were an influential group of professionals, including merchants and lawyers. In the 1620s, King Charles I forced hundreds of Puritan ministers to give up their positions. In 1630, about 900 Puritans formed the Massachusetts Bay Company and set sail for Massachusetts and New Hampshire. They were led by landowner and lawyer John Winthrop.

The Puritans believed their lives would be an example to others. Their main settlement was Boston, located on an excellent harbor. By 1643, about 20,000 colonists lived in the Massachusetts Bay Colony. By the mid-1630s, the colony had an elected assembly, the General Court, to which each town sent its representatives. Adult male Puritans elected the General Court and the colony's governor each year. Although they founded a colony in order to worship as they chose, the Puritans did not offer non-Puritans **toleration**, or recognition that other people have a right to different opinions.

Religious disputes led to new colonies. Roger Williams, minister of a church in Salem, believed that Puritans should leave the Church of England and that colonists should pay Native Americans for land, not seize it. Forced to leave Massachusetts Bay in 1635, he moved to Rhode Island. In 1644, colonists there received a charter of self-government from the king and decided that people of all faiths could worship as they chose.

(Continues on the next page.)

Lesson Vocabulary

persecute to mistreat or punish a group of people because of their beliefs

pilgrim an English settler who sought religious freedom in the Americas in the 1600s

toleration the willingness to let others practice their own beliefs

MODIFIED CORNELL NOTES

(Continued from page 14)

Anne Hutchinson, a Boston woman who questioned some Puritan concepts, was put on trial in 1638 and expelled from Massachusetts. She founded a settlement in Rhode Island. Thomas Hooker, a minister, left Massachusetts with one hundred followers in 1636 and founded Hartford, Connecticut. In 1639, the Fundamental Orders of Connecticut established a new government with an elected legislature and governor. In 1662, Connecticut received a charter granting it self-government. In 1638, John Wheelwright, who was forced out of Massachusetts for agreeing with some of Hutchinson's views, founded Exeter, New Hampshire. Massachusetts tried to control New Hampshire, but in 1680, the king made it a separate colony.

Puritans believed that towns and churches should govern themselves, and that people should work hard and live in stable families. Each Puritan town set up a **town meeting**, or an assembly of townspeople that decides local issues. New England families earned their living by farming, making leather and other goods, fishing, and shipbuilding. By the 1660s, 300 ships from New England were fishing off the coast or shipping goods across the Atlantic Ocean.

By the 1670s, the Native American population had fallen to 12,000, due to European diseases. In 1675, the chief of the Wampanoag, Metacom (also called King Philip), fought Puritan expansion. Some Native Americans supported him, but others helped the settlers. The fight, known as King Philip's War, killed thousands and destroyed 12 towns. In 1676, Metacom was killed. By then, a new generation born in America was focused on farming and business, not religion.

Lesson Vocabulary

town meeting a meeting in colonial New England where settlers discussed and voted on local government matters

TOPIC 2 LESSON 4

Lesson Summary
THE MIDDLE COLONIES

MODIFIED CORNELL NOTES

The Middle Colonies' soil and climate were conducive to farming. Quakers founded Pennsylvania and Delaware. People from many European countries settled in the Middle Colonies.

The Middle Colonies comprised four states: New York, New Jersey, Pennsylvania, and Delaware. New York was the largest and northernmost state. The Hudson River flows south through eastern New York. It empties into the Atlantic Ocean at New York City, which is today the most populous city in the country. New Jersey, just south of New York, is mostly lowland along the Atlantic coast. Pennsylvania is the region's second-largest state. Its largest city, Philadelphia, is located on the Delaware River on lowlands in the southeast. Delaware, the smallest state, is located south of New Jersey and also lies along the Atlantic coast.

The warmer, longer growing season and fertile soil made farming easier in the Middle Colonies than in New England. Farmers grew wheat, fruits, and vegetables.

New York was originally called New Netherland and was ruled by the Dutch. By 1660, Dutch farmers in the Hudson River valley prospered, and fur traders profited from dealing with Native Americans. The Dutch also made money trading with merchants in British colonies, which violated Britain's mercantile laws. The small ruling Dutch population felt hostility from other settlers. New Netherland blocked access between England's northern and southern colonies. In 1664, England's King Charles II granted the Dutch colonial land to his brother James, who conquered it. The colony was renamed New York, after James, the Duke of York. New Amsterdam, its capital, became New York City.

New Jersey was established in 1665, when part of southern New York was split off into a new colony. It began as a **proprietary colony**, or a colony created by a grant of land from a monarch to an individual or family. In 1702, however, it became a **royal colony**, a colony directly controlled by the English king. New York had become a royal colony in 1685.

(Continues on the next page.)

Lesson Vocabulary

proprietary colony an English colony in which the king gave land to proprietors in exchange for a yearly payment

royal colony a colony under direct control of the English crown

TOPIC 2 LESSON 4 — Lesson Summary
THE MIDDLE COLONIES

(Continued from page 16)

In the 1640s and 1650s, new religious groups emerged in England, including the Quakers, whose ideas set them apart from most groups. They believed that all people are equal, have a direct link with God, and therefore do not need ministers. By the 1660s, thousands of English Quakers refused to pay taxes to support the Church of England. To provide safety from persecution, William Penn, a wealthy Quaker leader, used his connections with King Charles II to get a charter for a new colony in North America. In 1681, he received an area nearly as large as England. Penn viewed his colony as a "holy experiment" to see if people from different religious backgrounds could live peacefully. In 1682, he wrote his Frame of Government for Pennsylvania, which granted the colony an elected assembly and freedom of religion. He did not allow colonists to settle on land until Native Americans sold it to them.

The first European settlers in Delaware were Swedish. The Dutch briefly took control but lost it along with New York to the English. Delaware settlers were averse to sending delegates to a distant Philadelphia. Penn gave the area its own assembly, and in 1704, Delaware became a separate colony.

By the 1700s, more than 20,000 colonists lived in Pennsylvania. Farmers produced a surplus. Because of its abundant wheat crop, Pennsylvania was called America's breadbasket. Manufacturers were appearing in the Middle Colonies, producing iron, flour, and paper. Artisans in towns included shoemakers, carpenters, masons, weavers, and coopers, who made barrels to ship and store flour and other foods. Pennsylvania's backcountry, or the frontier region extending from Pennsylvania to Georgia, was home to Scotch-Irish, and later, Germans. They called themselves *Deutsch* for "German" and became known as the Pennsylvania *Dutch*. By the 1750s, non-English settlers made the Middle Colonies the most diverse part of English North America.

Name_____ Class_____ Date_____

MODIFIED CORNELL NOTES

A farming region that required many laborers, the Southern Colonies depended on slavery. The Tidewater region and the backcountry developed two distinct ways of life.

In the 1760s, Charles Mason and Jeremiah Dixon drew the boundary known as the Mason-Dixon Line. After the American Revolution, it became the line between northern states where slavery was **banished** and southern states where it **persisted**. Maryland, Virginia, North Carolina, South Carolina, and Georgia were south of the line. They shared the Tidewater, a flat, coastal lowland with many swamps. The warm, humid climate provided a long growing season for tobacco and rice. Both crops required many field workers, which helped spread slavery.

In 1632, George Calvert, an English Catholic, set up a colony in Maryland where Catholics could live safely from discrimination. When he died, his son Cecil Calvert, Lord Baltimore, oversaw the colony along with a legislative assembly. Because of tension between Protestants and Catholics, Lord Baltimore got the assembly to pass the Act of Toleration in 1649. It welcomed all Christians and gave adult male Christians the right to vote and hold office.

The colony of Carolina was chartered in 1663. The northern part developed slowly because it lacked harbors and rivers for ships. Settlers lived on small farms and produced tobacco and lumber. The southern part grew quickly. Colonists used slave labor to grow sugar and rice in the swampy lowlands. Carolina became two colonies: North Carolina and South Carolina.

Georgia, the last of England's 13 colonies, was founded for two reasons. The English feared that Spain was expanding northward from its Florida colony. Also, wealthy Englishmen led by James Oglethorpe wanted a colony that would protect **debtors**, or people who owe money, from imprisonment. Oglethorpe banned slavery, but by the 1750s, it was legal.

In the 1700s, the Southern Colonies developed two distinct ways of life. Plantations, or large farms, dominated the economy in the Tidewater region. Tobacco and rice promoted the spread of slavery, until there were more slaves than free citizens in South Carolina. The plantation system made a society of slaveholders and enslaved people, and it divided wealthy landowners from poor people who lived in the backcountry. The backcountry was cut off from the coast by poor roads. Families lived in isolation. They believed the colonial government cared only about the wealthy, not them.

Lesson Vocabulary

banished put out or made illegal

persisted continued or remained unchanged

debtor a person who cannot pay money he or she owes

TOPIC 2
LESSON 6
Lesson Summary
COLONIAL SOCIETY

Although colonists had many differences, they were united by a common culture and faced many of the same daily challenges.

Many colonists came to America with the hope of owning land and building a better life. In England, land meant wealth, but most of the land was already owned by the upper classes. Social class in Europe was rigid, and those born poor had little opportunity to improve their status. In the colonies, however, land was available. There was also greater social equality in colonial America, although class distinctions still existed.

The **gentry** was the upper class of colonial society and included merchants, owners of large farms, royal officials, and lawyers. The gentry had great power and could often live in luxury.

The **middle class**, neither very rich nor very poor, included the great majority of colonists. These were the small planters, independent farmers, and artisans. Middle-class men could vote, and some held office. Most members of the middle class were white, although a small percentage were of African descent. Unlike in England, the poor could move upward socially and enter the middle class.

Puritan ideas influenced education in the colonies, and American literature began to be written. The religious movement was called the Great Awakening, and the intellectual ideas of the Enlightenment influenced American thought.

The first American literature was sermons and histories. Poetry developed slowly, beginning with America's first published poet, Anne Bradstreet. Published in 1650 after her death, Bradstreet's poems described the joys and hardships of life in Puritan New England. Phyllis Wheatley was an enslaved African in Boston, whose first poem was published in the 1760s when she was about 14. She wrote in an academic style that was popular in Europe.

Benjamin Franklin started writing for the *Pennsylvania Gazette* when he was 17. His most popular work, *Poor Richard's Almanack*, was published yearly from 1733 to 1753. He was also a scientist, businessman, inventor, and diplomat who became one of the founders of the United States.

(Continues on the next page.)

Lesson Vocabulary

gentry the highest social class in the English colonies

middle class in the English colonies, a class that included skilled craft workers, farmers, and some tradespeople

TOPIC 2 LESSON 6

Lesson Summary
COLONIAL SOCIETY

(Continued from page 19)

Religion was always a part of colonial life, but by the 1700s, rules on religion had become less strict in many of the colonies. This trend led to the Great Awakening, a strong Christian movement that swept through the colonies in the 1730s and 1740s. Jonathan Edwards was a Massachusetts preacher who called on people to commit themselves to God. Other preachers spread the movement on sermon tours, and the Great Awakening led to the rise of many new churches and sects. Methodist and Baptist membership grew quickly. Presbyterian, Dutch Reformed, and Congregationalist churches split into two groups: those who followed the Great Awakening and those who did not. The growth of new churches led to more tolerance of various religions and reinforced democratic ideas.

Puritans in New England combined education with religion. They passed laws requiring towns to provide schools. While public schools were supported by taxes, Puritan schools were supported by both public and private money. Colonial schools taught religion as well as reading, writing, and arithmetic. Most schools were in the North, where people lived more closely together. In the South, members of the gentry hired private tutors, while children of poorer families often received no education.

Only some schools admitted girls. **Dame schools** were opened by women to teach girls and boys to read. Enslaved Africans were not admitted to schools, although some Quaker and Anglican missionaries taught slaves to read.

After elementary school, some boys went to grammar school. The first American colleges were founded mainly to educate men for the ministry.

The Enlightenment was an intellectual movement that began in Europe in the late 1600s. Enlightenment thinkers believed that all problems could be solved by human reason. They looked for "natural laws" that governed politics, society, and economics. Englishman John Locke contributed some of the movement's key ideas.

The Zenger trial of 1735 helped to establish freedom of the press, or the right of journalists to publish the truth without restriction or penalty. Publisher John Peter Zenger was arrested for printing articles that criticized the governor of New York. Zenger was accused of **libel**, the publishing of statements that damage a person's reputation. The jury found Zenger not guilty, however, because the articles were based on fact.

Lesson Vocabulary

dame school a school run by women, usually in their own homes

libel the act of publishing a statement that may unjustly damage a person's reputation

Name_____ Class_____ Date_____

MODIFIED CORNELL NOTES

Under the theory of mercantilism, colonies existed to serve the economic needs of their parent country. In 1651, the English Parliament passed the first of several Navigation Acts to support mercantilism, an economic system that uses governmental regulation to improve a state at the expense of rival states. The laws required that any shipments bound for the colonies had to stop in England first. Any colonial shipments to England had to travel in British-owned ships. Colonies could sell tobacco, sugar, and other key products only to England. These laws benefited the colonies in many ways by providing a secure market. Yet many colonists resented the laws, which they felt limited the colonists' opportunities to make money by not being able to sell goods to foreign markets.

Between the 1500s and the 1800s, more than 10 million Africans were enslaved and brought to the Americas.

Slave traders developed a routine known as the **triangular trade**, a three-way trade between the colonies, the West Indies (islands of the Caribbean), and Africa:

- Ships from New England carried fish, lumber, and other goods to the West Indies. They returned with sugar and molasses, a syrup used to make rum.
- Ships from New England carried rum, guns, and other goods to West Africa, where they were traded for enslaved Africans.
- Ships from West Africa carried the slaves to the West Indies, where they were sold. With the profits, traders bought more molasses.

The triangular trade often disobeyed the Navigation Acts, which required colonists to buy goods only from English colonies.

(Continues on the next page.)

Lesson Vocabulary

mercantilism the theory that a nation's economic strength came from selling more than it bought from other nations

triangular trade the colonial trade route between New England, Africa, and the West Indies

Lesson Summary
COLONIAL TRADE AND GOVERNMENT

MODIFIED CORNELL NOTES

(Continued from page 21)

In 1215, King John signed the Magna Carta, the first document to limit the English monarch's power and protect the rights of nobles and other citizens. It also formed the basis for Parliament, a two-house **legislature**, or group of people who have the power to make laws. Parliament included two groups: the hereditary nobles of the House of Lords and the elected members of the House of Commons. The monarch needed the consent of Parliament to raise taxes—Parliament's greatest power. Conflict between King Charles I and Parliament led to the English Civil War in the 1640s. Charles I was executed by parliamentary forces. The monarchy was restored in 1660, yet Parliament retained its rights.

Parliament gained more power in 1688 when it removed King James I from the throne and replaced him with his daughter Mary and her husband William. After this so-called Glorious Revolution, the new monarchs signed the English Bill of Rights. A **bill of rights** is a written list of freedoms that a government promises to protect, including the right to a trial by jury.

The American colonists expected to receive many of the same rights that Englishmen possessed under parliamentary law. They set up legislatures, including the House of Burgesses in Jamestown and the General Court in Massachusetts. However, the British government gave William Penn full ownership of Pennsylvania. Penn and his council had the power to make laws. In 1701, colonists in Pennsylvania forced Penn to change the legal system so that only the General Assembly could make laws. By 1760, every colony had a legislature, although they frequently clashed with the colonial governors.

More white males could vote in the American colonies than in England. However, many groups could not vote, including women, Native Americans, and Africans.

Lesson Vocabulary

legislature a group of people who have the power to make laws

bill of rights a written list of freedoms the government promises to protect

Name_____ Class_____ Date_____

Answer the questions below using the information in the Lesson Summaries on the previous pages.

Lesson 1: Spanish Colonization and New Spain

1. Identify Who were the conquistadors, and what were they seeking?

_____

_____

2. How were the four levels of Spanish colonial society in North America based on birthplace and blood?

_____

_____

Lesson 2: The First French, Dutch, and English Colonies

3. Identify Cause and Effect Why did England, France, and Holland pay for voyages to North America?

_____

_____

4. In what ways did the House of Burgesses mark the start of representative government in North America?

_____

_____

Lesson 3: The New England Colonies

5. List List four colonists who had disagreements with some aspects of the Puritan religion, and name the places to which they moved.

_____

_____

6. Connect What did the Puritans believe about towns and churches, and what did Puritan towns establish as a result?

_____

_____

TOPIC 2 — Review Questions (continued)
EUROPEAN COLONIZATION OF NORTH AMERICA

Lesson 4: The Middle Colonies

7. Why were the Quakers persecuted in England?

_____

_____

8. **Explain** How did New Jersey's colonial status change in 1702?

_____

_____

Lesson 5: The Southern Colonies

9. What law was passed by Maryland's legislative assembly in 1649, and what did the law do?

_____

_____

10. **Contrast** How did the ways of life in the Tidewater region and the backcountry differ?

_____

_____

Lesson 6: Colonial Society

11. **Describe** How could people move up in class in colonial society?

_____

_____

12. What were two ideas held by Enlightenment thinkers?

_____

_____

Lesson 7: Colonial Trade and Government

13. **Analyze Information** What requirements of the Navigation Acts supported mercantilism?

_____

_____

14. What was the triangular trade, and which three regions did it connect?

_____

_____

TOPIC 3 — Note Taking Study Guide
THE REVOLUTIONARY ERA

Focus Question: The evolution of the United States as an independent, self-governing nation entailed many conflicts and fights along the way. In what situations were the act of fighting back, opposition, and war justified to meet this end? Explain which principles and rights Americans fought for during these events.

As you read the Lesson Summaries on the following pages, note specific examples of conflicts in the evolution of the United States as an independent, self-governing nation, and the principles or rights that justified the conflicts.

Conflict	Principle or Right

TOPIC
3
LESSON 1

Lesson Summary
THE FRENCH AND INDIAN WAR

MODIFIED CORNELL NOTES

Britain and France fought over North American territory. After several defeats, the British rallied to win the key battle of Quebec. The French **surrendered** their American territories to Britain and Spain.

France and Britain controlled large areas of North America by the mid-1700s. In 1753, the French began building forts to back their claim to the Ohio River valley. The Virginia Colony disputed France's claim. The governor of Virginia sent soldiers, led by a young George Washington, to build a fort where the Ohio River forms. But the French were already building Fort Duquesne (du KANE) at the spot. A large French army forced Washington and his men to return to Virginia.

At the request of the British government, colonial leaders met in Albany, New York. They discussed the war **looming** with France and a possible alliance with the Iroquois. An alliance is an agreement made between two countries to help each other. The Iroquois, believing the French had the stronger military advantage, chose not to ally with the British. At the meeting, Benjamin Franklin presented his Albany Plan of Union. Under this plan, colonial assemblies would elect a council that had authority over western settlements, as well as the power to organize armies and collect taxes to pay war expenses. The Albany Congress agreed to the plan, but the colonial assemblies, fearful of losing control of their taxes and armies, rejected it.

In 1755, the British government sent General Edward Braddock to push the French from the Ohio River valley. Braddock was not familiar with the fighting tactics of Native Americans in the wilderness. As Braddock's British troops and Virginia militia neared Fort Duquesne, the French and their Native American allies launched a crushing ambush. Braddock and more than half his men were killed. During this same year, the British colonials were also defeated at Fort Niagara and suffered heavy losses near Lake George.

In May 1756, Britain declared war on France—the official beginning of the Seven Years' War. Shortly after, the French captured two more British forts.

(Continues on the next page.)

Lesson Vocabulary

surrender to give up formally

looming impending or coming; hanging over

TOPIC 3
LESSON 1

Lesson Summary
THE FRENCH AND INDIAN WAR

(Continued from page 26)

MODIFIED CORNELL NOTES

When William Pitt became Britain's prime minister in 1757, he appointed **superior** generals whose talents were equal to the French challenge. This change of military command paid off. In 1758, the British captured the fort at Louisbourg and then Fort Duquesne. These two victories, followed by others, finally convinced the Iroquois to ally with the British. With growing confidence in their military strength, Britain prepared to attack the city of Quebec, the capital of New France.

The Battle of Quebec took place in September 1759. General James Wolfe led the British. The French were led by General Montcalm. The British won a key victory. Without Quebec, France could not defend the rest of its territories. In 1763, the two countries signed the Treaty of Paris. France ceded, or surrendered, almost all of its North American possessions to Britain and Spain.

Lesson Vocabulary
superior better or more capable

TOPIC 3 LESSON 2

Lesson Summary

TENSIONS WITH BRITAIN

MODIFIED CORNELL NOTES

By 1763, Britain controlled most of North America east of the Mississippi River. Native Americans within this region feared the encroachment of British settlers onto their lands. In May 1763, the Ottawa leader, Pontiac, attacked British forts and settlements. Many settlers were killed, and Britain retaliated. By August 1763, Pontiac's forces were defeated. Pontiac fought for another year, but by the fall of 1764, the war was over.

To avoid more conflicts, Britain issued the Proclamation of 1763. It banned colonial settlements west of the Appalachian Mountains. Many colonists felt the ban violated their right to live where they pleased. The ban was largely ignored.

The colonists were proud of their contribution to winning the French and Indian War. Although most colonists felt a degree of independence from Britain, they were still loyal British subjects. That loyalty began to erode when Britain, now deeply in debt from the French and Indian War, began to impose new taxes.

In 1764, Parliament passed the Sugar Act, which put a duty, or import tax, on several products, including molasses. Colonial merchants protested.

In 1765, Parliament passed the Stamp Act. This required colonists to buy special tax stamps to put on products, newspapers, and legal documents. In protest, some colonies passed a resolution declaring that only the colonial governments had the right to tax the colonists. Merchants in major cities **boycotted**, or refused to buy, British goods.

Finally, colonial delegates sent a **petition**, or a written request to the government, demanding an end to the Sugar Act and the Stamp Act. Parliament **repealed** the Stamp Act, but it passed the Declaratory Act, which said that Parliament had full authority over the colonies.

In 1767, Parliament passed the Townshend Acts, which declared that only products imported into the colonies would be taxed. To enforce these taxes, as well as to find smuggled goods, customs officers used **writs of assistance**. These legal documents allowed customs officers to make searches without saying what they were looking for.

(Continues on the next page.)

Lesson Vocabulary

boycott to refuse to buy or use certain goods or services

petition a formal written request to someone in authority that is signed by a group of people

repeal to cancel, remove from law

writ of assistance a legal document that allowed British customs officers to inspect a ship's cargo without giving a reason

Lesson Summary
TENSIONS WITH BRITAIN

(Continued from page 28)

Colonists boycotted British goods to protest this violation of their rights. Merchants in Britain suffered from the boycott. They pressured Parliament to repeal the Townshend duties, which it did— except for the tax on tea.

Then, on March 5, 1770, a small group of soldiers in Boston fired into an angry crowd, killing five citizens. After this incident, which became known as the Boston Massacre, Samuel Adams established a Committee of Correspondence in Massachusetts. Soon, other colonies set up committees. They wrote letters and pamphlets to keep colonists informed of British actions. This helped to unite the colonies.

Lesson Summary
TAKING UP ARMS

MODIFIED CORNELL NOTES

The colonists' protests over British policies continued to escalate until the British sent in troops to control the situation. This caused a confrontation that started the American Revolution.

Although most of the Townshend duties had been repealed, the tax on tea remained. Then, in 1773, Parliament passed the Tea Act. It gave the British East India Company a monopoly on British tea. This meant that the company had total control over all tea sold in the colonies. Although the Tea Act actually lowered the price of tea, it also kept colonial merchants from selling Dutch tea at competitive prices.

On the night of December 16, 1773, a large group of men disguised as Native Americans boarded the tea ship waiting in Boston Harbor. The ship's cargo of tea, worth thousands of dollars, was tossed into Boston Harbor. This event became known as the Boston Tea Party.

In response to the Boston Tea Party, the enraged British government passed harsh laws that the colonists called the Intolerable Acts. The laws closed the port of Boston, increased the powers of the royal governor, decreased the power of colonial self-government, and strengthened the Quartering Act. Parliament also passed the Quebec Act. This set up new Canadian boundaries that blocked colonists from moving west.

The First Continental Congress took place in Philadelphia in 1774. Delegates from all the colonies except Georgia participated. The Congress demanded that Parliament repeal, or officially end, the Intolerable Acts.

Britain rejected the demands of the First Continental Congress. It decided to restore its authority in the colonies by force. Anticipating this move, the colonists formed new **militias**. These were citizen soldiers who could serve during an emergency.

The British soldiers and the minutemen had their first confrontation in the town of Lexington, Massachusetts.

In July 1775, the Second Continental Congress sent two petitions to the king. The first one, called the Olive Branch Petition after an ancient symbol of peace, stated that the colonists were the king's loyal subjects. The second stated that the colonists were ready to fight for their freedom. The British Parliament ignored the Olive Branch Petition and voted to send 20,000 soldiers to the colonies to end the revolt.

(Continues on the next page.)

Lesson Vocabulary

militia an army of citizens who serve as soldiers during an emergency

Name_____ Class_____ Date_____

(Continued from page 30)

Like the delegates, the American people themselves were split in their loyalties. Farmers, workers, and many merchants who were affected by the new tax laws were willing to fight for independence. They were called **Patriots**. Those who owned property and held government positions had more to lose if America lost a war with Britain. These colonists, called **Loyalists**, remained loyal to the British monarchy in order to keep their lands and positions.

By June 1775, there were 6,500 British troops camped in Boston, while about 10,000 Americans surrounded the city. Nearly 1,600 of the colonial militia were atop Breed's Hill, which overlooked the city and the harbor. Nearby were more Americans on Bunker Hill. These colonial troops were farmers and workers, not trained soldiers. British General William Howe decided to attack straight up the hill. His first and second attacks failed, and many of his men were killed. His third attack succeeded, but only because the Americans ran out of ammunition. Although the British won this battle, known as the Battle of Bunker Hill, it proved that the Americans could successfully fight professional British soldiers.

Lesson Vocabulary
Patriot a colonist who favored war against Britain
Loyalist a colonist who remained loyal to Britain

Name_____ Class_____ Date_____

MODIFIED CORNELL NOTES

The first half of the year 1776 was marked by a major change in the colonists' thinking about their relationship with Britain. These months were also filled with actions by Patriots and delegates to the Continental Congress that led to a united and formal statement of independence.

At the beginning of 1776, few colonists were **inclined** to support a struggle for independence. Even in the Continental Congress, only one third of the delegates supported independence. The publication of Thomas Paine's *Common Sense*, however, marked the beginning of a shift in people's thinking. In May 1776, Richard Henry Lee presented to Congress a resolution, or formal statement of opinion, from his home state of Virginia on the right of the colonies to be free. Before voting on Lee's resolution, the Congress assigned a committee to write a formal statement listing reasons why the colonies should separate from Britain. The delegates chose Thomas Jefferson to draft the document.

Jefferson's **brilliance** as a writer is **evident** in the Declaration of Independence. The document has a logical flow through an introduction and three distinct sections.

Congress met in July 1776 to decide whether to adopt Lee's resolution and approve the Declaration of Independence. On July 4, 1776, the approval was announced. The Declaration was signed by the delegates on August 2. From that time forward, the Patriots were fighting to become an independent nation.

The Preamble, or introduction, explains why the document is being written.

The list of grievances states the formal complaints against King George III of England. He is accused of failing to protect the colonists' rights. Beyond that, the king is accused of actually violating their rights.

The Conclusion puts together the colonists' beliefs and grievances to show that the only course left to the colonists is to dissolve all political ties with Britain. An ending pledge demonstrates the seriousness of the colonists' Declaration of Independence.

Lesson Vocabulary
inclined tended toward

brilliance brightness; high ability

evident clearly seen, obvious

Lesson Summary

TOPIC 3 LESSON 5

WINNING INDEPENDENCE

The early years of the war included **significant** losses as well as victories for the Continental Army. Help came in surprising ways to cause the tide to turn in favor of the Americans.

By mid-1776, the war shifted from Boston and New England to the Middle Colonies. In New York, the Continental Army did not fare well against the British. Led by Sir William Howe, 34,000 British troops and 10,000 sailors attacked the much smaller and less experienced American forces on Long Island. Washington and his soldiers were forced to retreat from Long Island to New York City, then north to White Plains, and eventually west and south through New Jersey. Nathan Hale was an American hero who emerged as a legend from these difficult times. He volunteered to spy on the British at Long Island, but he was caught behind British lines and hanged. His famous last words were, "I only regret that I have but one life to lose for my country."

By December 1776, the Continental Army had retreated all the way into Pennsylvania. The soldiers' spirits **plunged** as they failed to achieve any victories. Some soldiers even began to desert the army. Thomas Paine wrote The Crisis to inspire soldiers to remain committed to the cause of freedom.

On Christmas night, Washington led his soldiers across the Delaware River for a surprise attack on Trenton from two sides. The defeated troops were Hessian **mercenaries**, or soldiers who are paid to fight for a country other than their own. Another American attack near Princeton boosted morale throughout the army.

British General John Burgoyne developed a plan that he thought would quickly defeat the Americans. He designed a three-pronged attack to cut off New England from the other colonies. King George III, however, issued orders that interfered with this plan, and American troops rushed to block British movements. By September 1777, American General Horatio Gates had 6,000 men ready to fight. On October 17, 1777, they forced Burgoyne and his troops to surrender in Saratoga, New York. This victory secured the New England Colonies for the Americans, lifted the Patriots' spirits, and showed Europe that the Continental Army might be able to win the war.

(Continues on the next page.)

Lesson Vocabulary

significant important or large

plunge to fall to a low point

mercenary soldier who is paid to fight for a country other than his own

TOPIC 3 LESSON 5

Lesson Summary

WINNING INDEPENDENCE

(Continued from page 33)

MODIFIED CORNELL NOTES

Many women supported the war effort. Some joined their husbands at the front, taking care of the wounded, washing clothes, and cooking. Others fought in battles. As a result, women began to think differently about their rights.

Through the bitter winter of 1777–1778, Washington and his troops suffered terribly at Valley Forge, Pennsylvania. The army was undersupplied, with shortages in food, clothing, and medicine. Drafty huts could not keep out the chill. About one fourth of the soldiers were sick at any given time. Nevertheless, the soldiers gathered their strength and sharpened their skills for the battles to come.

Both free and enslaved African Americans were soldiers from the beginning of the war. The British offered freedom to all enslaved people who would serve on their side. Americans at first blocked African Americans from service in the army. Washington changed this policy after seeing how many African Americans joined the British cause. By the end of the war, some 7,000 African Americans had joined the American armed forces. Most southern colonies still kept African Americans out of state armies for fear of slave revolts, but several northern colonies made moves to end slavery during the Revolutionary War.

Topic 3 — Review Questions

THE REVOLUTIONARY ERA

Answer the questions below using the information in the Lesson Summaries on the previous pages.

Lesson 1: The French and Indian War

1. What were the provisions of the Albany Plan of Union?

_____

_____

2. Sequence Events After William Pitt became Britain's prime minister in 1757, what series of military events led to the British victory?

_____

_____

Lesson 2: Tensions with Britain

3. Explain Why did Britain impose the Sugar Act and the Stamp Act?

_____

_____

4. How did the Committees of Correspondence help to unite the colonists?

_____

_____

Lesson 3: Taking Up Arms

5. Identify Cause and Effect What event prompted the British to pass the Intolerable Acts?

_____

_____

6. What did the First Continental Congress accomplish?

_____

_____

Lesson 4: Declaring Independence

7. What two things happened to bring the colonists and the Congress closer to a formal call for independence?

_____

_____

8. Identify Central Ideas What did the signing of the Declaration of Independence mean for the colonists?

_____

_____

Lesson 5: Winning Independence

9. Identify Cause and Effect What were the effects of the Battle of Saratoga?

_____

_____

10. What were the conditions at Valley Forge during the winter of 1777–1778, and how did the troops respond?

_____

_____

Name_____ Class_____ Date_____

TOPIC 4

Note Taking Study Guide
A CONSTITUTION FOR THE UNITED STATES

Focus Question: After gaining independence, how did the newly formed government of the United States protect the rights and liberties of its citizens? In what ways did the government deny equality and freedom to Americans?

As you read the Lesson Summaries on the following pages, note specific examples of ways in which the newly formed government of the United States protected citizens' rights and liberties and ways in which it denied equality and freedom.

Rights and Liberties of Citizens	
Protected	**Denied**
•	•

TOPIC 4 LESSON 1

Lesson Summary
A WEAK CONFEDERATION

MODIFIED CORNELL NOTES

Many of the former colonies wrote new state **constitutions**. A constitution is a document stating the rules under which government will operate. Most states minimized the power of state governors because colonial governors had abused their power. Instead, most power was given to the state legislature, the lawmaking body elected by the people.

The new state constitutions allowed more people to vote. In most states, white men 21 years or older could vote if they owned some property, but women and African Americans were not allowed to vote. Virginia was the first state to have a bill of rights, which is a list of essential freedoms that the government is required to respect.

The Continental Congress created the Articles of Confederation in 1777. This plan created a new national government for the United States with restricted powers.

The national government had a single branch, a one-house legislature called Congress, which had the power to pass laws, deal with foreign nations and Native Americans, make war and peace, coin or borrow money, and run a post office. Congress was not given the power to collect taxes or to **interfere** with trade between the states. All states were equal, and most power remained in the hands of the states.

Under the Articles of Confederation, the United States won its independence, negotiated a peace treaty with Britain, and created rules for settling new territories. There were also problems: trade **rivalries** and taxation between states hurt the economy, the national government was too weak to stop public **unrest**, and it had little money because it could not collect taxes.

The Land Ordinance of 1785 created a way for national lands to be sold to the public. It divided public western lands into square townships of six miles on each side. This would result in a grid of squares. Within each township, there would also be a grid, one mile on each side. Each township had one section that was set aside to support schools. This reflected the belief of the nation's leaders that democracy depended on education.

(Continues on the next page.)

Lesson Vocabulary

constitution a document that sets out the laws, principles, organization, and processes of a government

interfere to disturb or change without permission

rivalry competition or struggle, often unfriendly, between two entities

unrest dissatisfaction; public protest, often violent

TOPIC **4**
LESSON 1

Lesson Summary
A WEAK CONFEDERATION

(Continued from page 38)

A law called the Northwest Ordinance of 1787 applied to the territory north of the Ohio River. It guaranteed basic rights to settlers, outlawed slavery, and established a process for creating new states in the territory. Eventually, five states would be settled in the Northwest Territory.

During the mid-1780s, hard economic times in Massachusetts caused many farmers to lose their land because they could not pay their taxes. In Shays' Rebellion, a group of Massachusetts farmers rose up against the state in protest. The rebellion failed, but it led to calls for a stronger national government.

Lesson Summary
DRAFTING A CONSTITUTION

MODIFIED CORNELL NOTES

The Constitutional Convention met in Philadelphia in 1787. At the start, the delegates agreed to hold discussions in secret so that there would be less public pressure. The Convention's initial purpose was to revise the Articles of Confederation, but soon its members agreed that revising the Articles was not enough. The 55 delegates, representing 12 states, included respected leaders of the Revolution. George Washington was quickly voted president of the Convention.

From the start, an entirely new framework of government was proposed. James Madison wrote the Virginia Plan, which called for a strong central government with three branches instead of one. The **judicial branch** would consist of a system of courts to settle disputes involving national issues, and an **executive branch** would carry out the laws. It was agreed that the executive branch would have one chief executive, called the President.

Congress would remain the **legislative branch**. However, the Virginia Plan sought to change Congress. It added a second house and made it so each state would be represented in the two houses based on its population. The more people a state had, the more seats it would have in each house. This idea drew support from big states like Virginia, Pennsylvania, and Massachusetts.

States with small populations opposed the changes in the legislative branch and offered their own plan called the New Jersey Plan. It called for a single house of Congress where all the states would have equal representation.

The Great Compromise settled the disagreement between the large and small states. A **compromise** is an agreement in which each side gives up part of what it wants. To please the large states, the House of Representatives was developed. Each state's representation in the House would be based on population, and its members would serve two-year terms. In the Senate, which was formed to please the small states, each state would have two senators serving six-year terms.

(Continues on the next page.)

Lesson Vocabulary

judicial branch a branch of government that decides if laws are carried out fairly

executive branch a branch of government that carries out laws

legislative branch a branch of government that passes laws

compromise a settlement or peaceful solution in which each side gives up some of its demands in order to reach an agreement or peaceful solution

TOPIC 4 LESSON 2

Lesson Summary

DRAFTING A CONSTITUTION

(Continued from page 40)

MODIFIED CORNELL NOTES

The Great Compromise was a vital step in creating a new Constitution. Now, small-state delegates were willing to support a strong central government.

Slavery also divided the Convention. The southern states, where there were more slaves, wanted slaves to count toward representation in the House. Northerners argued that slaves, who were not allowed to vote, should not be counted. It was agreed that each slave would count as three fifths of a person. This was called the Three-Fifths Compromise.

The Three-Fifths Compromise was a gain for the South, which got more seats in the House. Northern delegates reluctantly agreed in order to keep the South in the Union.

A second dispute arose when northern delegates called for a total ban on the buying and selling of slaves. A compromise was reached whereby the importation of slaves from other countries could be banned in 20 years, but there would be no restrictions on the slave trade within the United States.

The Constitution was submitted to the states, and each state called a convention to decide whether to ratify, or approve, the Constitution. At least nine states had to ratify the Constitution or it would not go into effect.

Lesson Summary
IDEAS THAT INFLUENCED THE CONSTITUTION

MODIFIED CORNELL NOTES

In drafting the Constitution, the Framers used ideas and principles from a variety of historical documents and important thinkers of Europe.

Enlightenment thinkers John Locke and Baron de Montesquieu were also key influences. Locke declared that every person has a natural right to life, liberty, and property. Montesquieu suggested the concept of separation of powers. **Separation of powers** states that the powers of government must be clearly defined and divided into legislative, executive, and judicial branches.

The delegates to the Constitutional Convention were influenced by past experiments with democracy and natural rights. American leaders looked to the ancient Roman Republic as a model. A **republic** is a government in which citizens rule themselves through elected representatives.

The following principles from the Magna Carta and the English Bill of Rights influenced the United States Constitution:

- Citizens have rights, which the government must protect.
- Even the head of the government must obey the law.
- Taxes cannot be raised without the consent of the people.
- Elections should be held frequently.
- People accused of crimes have the right to trial by jury and the right of **habeas corpus**, meaning no person may be held in prison without being charged with a specific crime.
- People have the right to private property, or property owned by an individual.

Lesson Vocabulary

separation of powers a principle by which the powers of government are divided among separate branches

republic a system of government in which citizens choose representatives to govern them

habeas corpus the right not to be held in prison without first being charged with a specific crime

TOPIC 4
LESSON 4

Lesson Summary
FEDERALISTS, ANTIFEDERALISTS, AND THE BILL OF RIGHTS

MODIFIED CORNELL NOTES

After the 1787 Convention, the Constitution was sent to the states for approval. Its opponents and supporters debated energetically, and after the Bill of Rights was added, all the states approved the Constitution.

The Federalists wanted a strong federal, or national, government. Three important Federalist leaders—Alexander Hamilton, John Jay, and James Madison—wrote a series of 85 newspaper essays called the *Federalist Papers* in support of the Constitution.

At the heart of the Federalist position was the need for a stronger central government. The Federalists argued that in order for the Union to last, the national government had to have powers denied it under the Articles of Confederation, including the power to enforce laws.

The opponents of the Constitution were known as Antifederalists. Many Antifederalists, such as George Mason and Patrick Henry, agreed that the Articles of Confederation were not strong enough. However, they felt that the Constitutional Convention had gone too far.

At least nine states had to **ratify** the Constitution or it would not go into effect. Delaware acted first. Its convention approved the Constitution in December 1787. Pennsylvania, New Jersey, Georgia, and Connecticut followed close behind.

The Federalists' strong efforts in Massachusetts led to approval in that state despite opposition in rural areas from which Shays' Rebellion had drawn its strength. By then, Maryland and South Carolina had ratified, which made a total of eight state ratifications. Then, in June 1788, New Hampshire became the ninth state to ratify the Constitution, meaning it could now go into effect. The other states eventually approved the Constitution, with Rhode Island being the last of the original 13 states to do so in May 1790.

After nine states had ratified the Constitution, Congress took steps to prepare for a presidential election. George Washington was elected the first President, with John Adams as Vice President.

During the debate on the Constitution, many states had insisted that a bill of rights be added. This became one of the first tasks of the new Congress that met in March 1789.

(Continues on the next page.)

Lesson Vocabulary
ratify officially approve

TOPIC 4 — LESSON 4

Lesson Summary
FEDERALISTS, ANTIFEDERALISTS, AND THE BILL OF RIGHTS

MODIFIED CORNELL NOTES

(Continued from page 43)

In 1789, Congress passed a series of **amendments**, or changes to a document. By December 1791, three fourths of the states had ratified 10 amendments. These amendments are known as the Bill of Rights.

The Bill of Rights protects citizens against governmental abuses of power. The First Amendment protects freedom of religion, speech, and the press.

The Third Amendment bars Congress from forcing citizens to keep troops in their homes, as Britain had done. The Fourth Amendment protects citizens from **unreasonable** searches of their homes or seizure of their property.

Lesson Vocabulary

amendment formal change to a document

unreasonable beyond what is normal; without basis

TOPIC 4
LESSON 5

Lesson Summary
UNDERSTANDING THE CONSTITUTION

The Preamble, or opening statement, of the Constitution outlines the goals of the document. Seven sections called the Articles make up the main body of the Constitution. The first three Articles describe the branches of government: legislative, executive, and judicial. Article 4 requires states to honor one another's laws and sets up a system for admitting new states. Article 5 provides a process for amending the Constitution. Article 6 declares the Constitution the "supreme law of the land." Article 7 sets up the procedure for the states to ratify the Constitution. In more than 200 years, only 27 changes have been made to the Constitution.

The Constitution rests on seven basic principles:

- **Popular sovereignty** asserts that the people are the main source of the government's authority.
- **Limited government** means the government only has powers given to it by the Constitution.
- Separation of powers divides the federal government into three branches. Each branch has its own duties.
- **Checks and balances** is a system by which each branch of government has the power to limit the actions of the other two. Like the separation of powers, this is designed to prevent the abuse of power.
- **Federalism** is the division of power between the federal government and the states.
- Republicanism provides for a government in which people elect representatives to carry out their will.
- The principle of individual rights means the Constitution protects rights such as freedom of speech and the right to trial by jury.

(Continues on the next page.)

Lesson Vocabulary

popular sovereignty government by consent of the governed

limited government a principle of the United States Constitution that states that government has only the powers that the Constitution gives it

checks and balances a principle of the United States Constitution that gives each branch of government the power to check, or limit, the other branches

federalism a principle of the United States Constitution that establishes the division of power between the federal government and the states

Name_____ Class_____ Date_____

MODIFIED CORNELL NOTES

(Continued from page 45)

The federal government consists of three branches, each of which has its own unique powers and responsibilities.

Article 1 of the Constitution sets up the Congress to make the nation's laws. Congress consists of two bodies: the Senate and the House of Representatives.

The Senate is based on equal representation and includes two senators from each state. Senators serve six-year terms. The Vice President serves as the president of the Senate.

The House of Representatives is the larger of the two bodies. Representation in the House is based on a state's population. People elect their representatives for two-year terms. The leader of the House, called the Speaker, regulates debates and agendas in the House.

The most important power Congress has is the power to make the nation's laws. A law starts as a **bill**, or proposal, which can be introduced in either the House or the Senate. Congress can also collect taxes, coin money, establish post offices, fix standard weights and measures, and declare war.

Much of the work in Congress is done through committees. Each committee deals with a specific topic, such as defense, education, or science.

Article 2 of the Constitution sets up the executive branch to carry out laws and to run the affairs of the national government. The President is the head of the executive branch, which also includes the Vice President and the Cabinet. The people in the many departments and agencies are also part of the executive branch. The Framers of the Constitution intended Congress to be the most powerful branch of government. Therefore, while the Constitution is very specific about the powers of the legislature, it offers few details about the powers of the President. Beginning with George Washington, Presidents have taken the actions they thought were necessary to meet the nation's changing needs. Today, the President can veto bills, propose laws, grant pardons, appoint high officials, negotiate treaties, and serve as commander in chief of the armed forces.

(Continues on the next page.)

Lesson Vocabulary
bill a proposed law

TOPIC 4
LESSON 5

Lesson Summary
UNDERSTANDING THE CONSTITUTION

(Continued from page 46)

The President serves a four-year term and cannot serve more than two terms. The President is elected through a system called the **electoral college**. Americans do not directly elect the President; rather, they vote for a group of electors. The number of electors depends on each state's number of senators and representatives. In most states, the presidential candidate with the majority of popular votes receives all of that state's electoral votes. The candidate who receives the most electoral votes becomes President.

The Constitution also established a Supreme Court and authorizes Congress to establish other courts that are needed. The system of federal courts was set up under the Judiciary Act of 1789.

Most federal cases begin in district courts, where evidence is presented and a judge or a jury decides the facts of a case. If a party disagrees with the decision of the judge or jury, it may appeal. An **appeal** asks that the decision be reviewed by a higher court. A judge in an appellate court, or court of appeals, reviews the decision to determine if the lower court interpreted and applied the law correctly.

The Supreme Court is at the top of the judicial branch, and it consists of a chief justice and eight associate justices. The President nominates the justices, and Congress must approve the appointments. The Supreme Court is the final court of appeals. Decisions rest on a majority of at least five of the justices.

There is no court of appeals beyond the Supreme Court. However, the Supreme Court may sometimes reverse its own past decisions.

The most important power of the Supreme Court is the power to decide what the Constitution means. The Court can declare whether acts of the President or laws passed by Congress are unconstitutional. **Unconstitutional** means that an act or law is not allowed by the Constitution.

(Continues on the next page.)

Lesson Vocabulary

electoral college a group of electors from each state who are chosen by voters every four years to vote for the President and Vice President of the United States

appeal to ask that a decision be reviewed by a higher court

unconstitutional not permitted by the Constitution

Lesson Summary
UNDERSTANDING THE CONSTITUTION

MODIFIED CORNELL NOTES

(Continued from page 47)

The Framers believed the separation of powers and checks and balances would prevent the rise of a single powerful leader or branch of government. For example, the President had the ability to **veto**, or reject, bills passed by Congress. Similarly, Congress could **override**, or overrule, the veto.

Under the principle of federalism, the Constitution divides powers between the federal government and the governments of states. In general, the federal government deals with national issues. The states concern themselves with local needs.

The Constitution identifies the powers of the federal and state government, but it says nothing about **local government**, which consists of smaller units such as counties, cities, and towns.

Lesson Vocabulary

veto to reject, as when the President rejects a law passed by Congress

override to overrule, as when Congress overrules a presidential veto

local government a government on the county, parish, city, town, village, or district level

TOPIC 4 LESSON 6

Lesson Summary
AMENDING THE CONSTITUTION

MODIFIED CORNELL NOTES

The founders created a Constitution that allowed for change. The first 10 changes made to the Constitution concerned the rights of the American people.

Some of the Framers were **dissatisfied** with the Constitution because the final document did not address the rights of the American people. The Framers fixed the **omission** by adding the Bill of Rights, the first 10 amendments to the Constitution. Such an addition was possible because the Constitution included Article 5, which laid out the method of amending the Constitution. *Amending* is another word for changing the Constitution. The Constitution can be changed in one of four ways. There are two ways of proposing an amendment. First, Congress can propose an amendment. Second, state legislatures can call for a national convention to propose an amendment.

An amendment can be ratified or approved through the actions of the state legislatures, or it can be ratified through the actions of state conventions. Conventions are special meetings that are called to address a specific issue.

The first 10 amendments, also known as the Bill of Rights, make up the part of the Constitution that addresses the freedoms guaranteed to all citizens.

The First Amendment affirms freedom of religion as a basic right. Americans are free to follow any religion or no religion at all. It is their choice.

The First Amendment also protects the right of Americans to speak without fear of punishment.

Since the addition of the Bill of Rights, the Constitution has been amended only 17 times. However, some of these amendments brought about drastic changes. The Thirteenth Amendment **abolished** slavery, and the Nineteenth Amendment gave women the right to vote. The Twenty-sixth Amendment lowered the minimum voting age to 18.

Lesson Vocabulary

dissatisfied not satisfied; unhappy

omission something that is left out; oversight

abolish to make illegal; to end officially

TOPIC 4 LESSON 7

Lesson Summary
CITIZENS' RIGHTS AND RESPONSIBILITIES

A **citizen** is someone who is entitled to all the rights and privileges of a nation. To be a citizen of the United States, a person must be born in the United States, have a parent who is a United States citizen, be naturalized, or be 18 years old or younger when his or her parents are naturalized. **Naturalization** is the official legal process of becoming a citizen. To be naturalized, a person must live in the United States for at least five years. The person must then apply for citizenship, take a citizenship exam, undergo interviews, and, finally, take the citizenship oath before a judge. In this oath, the person swears to "support and defend the Constitution and laws of the United States."

A naturalized citizen enjoys every right of a natural-born citizen except one. Only natural-born citizens may serve as President or Vice President.

The law holds citizens to certain responsibilities. For example, every citizen must obey the law and pay taxes—or face legal punishment. Good citizens meet other responsibilities as well. These are not required by law, but they are important. These responsibilities include learning about important issues, participating on juries, and voting in federal, state, and local elections.

Lesson Vocabulary

citizen a person who owes loyalty to a particular nation and is entitled to all its rights and protections

naturalization the process of granting citizenship to a person who has met official requirements for becoming a citizen

Name_____ Class_____ Date_____

Answer the questions below using the information in the Lesson Summaries on the previous pages.

Lesson 1: A Weak Confederation

1. Why were the state and national governments' powers limited?

_____

_____

2. Classify What were the successes and problems of the national government under the Articles of Confederation?

_____

_____

Lesson 2: Drafting a Constitution

3. What were the three branches of government proposed by the Virginia Plan?

_____

_____

4. Identify Central Issues What two main issues about slavery divided the northern and southern states during the Constitutional Convention?

_____

_____

Lesson 3: Ideas That Influenced the Constitution

5. Check Understanding What was Montesquieu's idea of the separation of powers?

_____

_____

6. Name two documents from British history that influenced the Constitution.

_____

_____

Lesson 4: Federalists, Antifederalists, and the Bill of Rights

7. Compare and Contrast How were the views of the Federalists and Antifederalists similar, and how did they differ?

_____

_____

TOPIC 4

Review Questions (continued)
A CONSTITUTION FOR THE UNITED STATES

8. What role did the Bill of Rights play in the debate on the Constitution?

_____

_____

Lesson 5: Understanding the Constitution

9. What is described in the first three Articles of the Constitution?

_____

_____

10. **Identify Central Ideas** List three of the basic principles embodied in the Constitution.

_____

_____

Lesson 6: Amending the Constitution

11. **Explain** Explain the two ways by which an amendment to the Constitution can be ratified.

_____

_____

12. **Make Generalizations** What is the overall focus of the Bill of Rights?

_____

_____

Lesson 7: Citizens' Rights and Responsibilities

13. What is required for a person to be a citizen of the United States?

_____

_____

14. **List** Name three responsibilities of citizens.

_____

_____

Name_____ Class_____ Date_____

Focus Question: In the early 1800s, Americans felt a growing sense of pride in their new nation. How did this feeling help Americans define their identity as a people? What obstacles did they face in developing this national identity?

As you read the Lesson Summaries on the following pages, note specific examples of sources of pride in the development of a national identity and examples of obstacles to that development.

Development of a National Identity	
Sources of Pride	**Obstacles**
•	•

Lesson Summary
WASHINGTON'S PRESIDENCY

MODIFIED CORNELL NOTES

As the first President, George Washington set many **precedents**, or examples to be followed by others in the future. He created new federal departments. The heads of these departments made up the **Cabinet**. Alexander Hamilton led the Treasury, Thomas Jefferson led the State Department, Henry Knox was Secretary of War, and Edmund Randolph was Attorney General. The group came to be called the Cabinet. In addition, the Judiciary Act of 1789 established a federal court system headed by the Supreme Court.

The American Revolution had left the nation deeply in debt. The debt was mainly in the form of bonds. A **bond** is a certificate issued by a government for an amount of money that the government promises to pay back with interest. Most of the original buyers sold their bonds to **speculators**, people who invest in a risky venture in the hope of making a large profit. Because speculators bought the bonds for less than they were worth, it did not seem fair to pay them in full, especially since the original bondholders had lost money. The government also questioned whether or not it should pay back state debts.

It fell to Alexander Hamilton, the new Secretary of the Treasury, to come up with a plan to solve the financial crisis. The first part of his plan was for the government to pay back all federal and state debts. However, many southern states did not want the federal government to pay state debts because they had paid theirs on their own. The South eventually agreed to this part of Hamilton's plan, and in return, the government would build its capital in the South.

The second part of the plan was to charter a national bank for depositing government funds. Members of Washington's Cabinet fought over whether the government had the right to do this.

(Continues on the next page.)

Lesson Vocabulary

precedent an act or decision that sets an example for others to follow

Cabinet the group of officials who head government departments and advise the President

bond a certificate that promises to repay money loaned, plus interest, on a certain date

speculator someone who invests in a risky venture in the hope of making a large profit

Lesson Summary
WASHINGTON'S PRESIDENCY

(Continued from page 54)

MODIFIED CORNELL NOTES

Southerners also opposed the last part of Hamilton's plan—a national **tariff**, or a tax on imported goods. The tariff benefited northern industries because it protected them from lower-priced foreign goods. Since southerners had little industry, the tariff only hurt them by raising prices. Congress did not pass the tariff.

Congress imposed a tax on all whiskey made and sold in the country, but many farmers who made whiskey opposed this tax. Some Pennsylvania farmers started a violent protest called the Whiskey Rebellion. Washington sent federal troops to Pennsylvania, showing that armed rebellion would not be accepted.

When the French Revolution began in 1789, Americans supported the effort of the French people to overthrow their king. By 1793, however, growing violence in France was becoming controversial in the United States, and it led Federalists to oppose the revolution. Republicans continued to support it, arguing that some violence could be expected in a fight for freedom.

By 1793, Britain and France were at war. Republicans supported France, and Federalists supported Britain. President Washington issued a proclamation that said the United States would remain **neutral**, not favoring either side of the dispute.

Washington sent John Jay to negotiate a treaty with Britain. In 1795, Jay returned with a treaty. The United States agreed to pay debts owed to British merchants. Britain agreed to pay for the ships it had seized and to withdraw its troops from the Northwest Territory. But it refused to stop impressing sailors. It also refused to recognize a U.S. right to trade with France.

Washington published his Farewell Address at the end of his second term. He advised Americans to avoid political divisions at home. He feared that violent divisions might tear the nation apart. Washington also emphasized his belief that the United States must stay out of European affairs. Washington's main accomplishments were establishing a federal government, ending the country's economic crisis, forcing the British to leave the Northwest Territory, and keeping the country out of war.

Lesson Vocabulary

tariff a tax on foreign goods brought into a country

neutral not taking sides in a conflict

MODIFIED CORNELL NOTES

The Framers of the Constitution did not expect political parties to form in the United States. Rather, they thought that government leaders would rise above personal or local interests and work together for the sake of the whole nation. They proved to be wrong.

In those days, people spoke of *factions* rather than *political parties*. A **faction** was an organized political group, and the word was not complimentary. James Madison thought factions were selfish groups that ignored the well-being of the whole nation. In *The Federalist*, he wrote than an effective national government would prevent the growth of factions. President Washington feared the effects of factions and tried to discourage their growth. Despite his efforts, by the early 1790s, political parties began to form.

The two parties that formed were called the Republicans and the Federalists. The Republicans developed out of Democratic-Republican clubs that accused the federal government of growing too strong. They wanted to keep most power at the state or local level. The Federalists took their name from the people who had supported the **adoption** of the Constitution. They believed that the United States needed a strong federal government to hold the country together.

At the time that both parties were organizing, the Federalists had an advantage. This was because President Washington usually supported Alexander Hamilton and his policies rather than Thomas Jefferson and his policies. Finally, in 1793, Jefferson resigned as Secretary of State because he was unhappy with the federal government's support of Federalist policies.

George Washington announced he would not run for a third term as President. His action set an important precedent. Not until Franklin Roosevelt ran for and won a third term in 1940 would any President seek more than two terms. In 1951, the Twenty-second Amendment limited the President to two terms.

Today, the President and Vice President run together on the same ticket. However, at the time of the 1796 election, the President and the Vice President were not elected as a ticket. The candidate with the most votes became President, and the candidate who came in second place was elected Vice President. In the 1796 election, a Federalist, John Adams, became President, but a Republican candidate, Thomas Jefferson, was elected Vice President. Not surprisingly, this led to serious tensions during the next four years.

Lesson Vocabulary

faction a party, or an opposing group within a party

adoption acceptance or approval; putting into effect

Lesson Summary
JOHN ADAMS'S PRESIDENCY

MODIFIED CORNELL NOTES

The decision of the United States to remain neutral during the war between France and Britain angered France because it had been an ally during the American Revolution. Also, the signing of Jay's Treaty with Britain made it appear as if the United States favored Britain over France. As a result, France refused to meet with an American diplomat and continued to seize American ships.

In 1797, Adams sent three diplomats to France. Agents of the French foreign minister demanded a bribe from the American diplomats, but the Americans refused to pay one. Many Americans, especially Federalists, were outraged when they learned of the so-called XYZ Affair. (XYZ refers to the three French agents whose real names were kept secret.)

The XYZ Affair led to an undeclared naval war with France. Adams and the Congress increased the size of the army and rebuilt the navy. In addition, Adams created a new department of the navy.

Adams, who opposed war, sent another group of diplomats to France. In 1800, a treaty was signed. France agreed to stop seizing American ships, and the United States avoided a full-scale war with France. The treaty angered many of Adams's fellow Federalists who wanted war with France.

The undeclared war with France increased distrust between the Federalists and Republicans. Federalists feared that European immigrants would spread dangerous ideas inspired by the French Revolution to America. They also feared that the new immigrants would favor the pro-French Republican Party when they became citizens.

The Federalist-controlled Congress decided to pass several laws. Its members had two main goals. First, they wanted to slow the process of becoming a citizen. Second, they wanted to stop immigrants and Republicans from spreading ideas that threatened Federalist control of the federal government.

The Alien Act increased the length of time it took for an **alien**, or someone from another country, to become a citizen from 5 to 14 years. It also allowed the President to jail or deport aliens he considered dangerous.

(Continues on the next page.)

Lesson Vocabulary
alien someone from another country

MODIFIED CORNELL NOTES

(Continued from page 57)

The Sedition Act targeted Republicans. **Sedition** is an activity aimed at overthrowing a government. The act made saying or writing anything insulting or false about the government a crime punishable by jail or a fine. The Sedition Act placed the harshest limits on free speech in the country's history. During 1798 and 1799, 10 people were convicted under the act. Most were Republican editors and printers.

Republicans denounced the Alien and Sedition Acts. They declared that the Sedition Act violated free speech protections under the First Amendment of the Constitution. However, it had not yet been clearly established that the Supreme Court had the power to strike down a law as unconstitutional. To overturn this law, therefore, the Republicans worked through state legislatures.

James Madison and Thomas Jefferson wrote resolutions for the Virginia and Kentucky legislatures, respectively. They stated that states had the right to declare federal laws unconstitutional.

The Virginia and Kentucky resolutions had little short-term impact. No other states supported them. By 1802, the Alien and Sedition Acts had expired, and Congress restored the waiting period for citizenship to five years.

The resolutions were far more important in the long run because they established the principles of **states' rights** and nullification. States' rights is the idea that the union binding "these United States" is an agreement among the states and that they therefore can overrule federal law. Nullification is the related idea that states have the power to **nullify**, or deprive of legal force, a federal law. These ideas increased in importance when the southern states began defending slavery.

The presidential campaign of 1800 was a bitter contest between the Federalists and the Republicans. The Federalists threatened a civil war if Jefferson won the election. Thomas Jefferson, the Republican candidate, received 73 electoral votes, defeating John Adams, the Federalist candidate. According to the Constitution, the person who received the next highest total of electoral votes would become Vice President. However, Aaron Burr, Jefferson's running mate, also received 73 votes. It was up to the House of Representatives to break the tie. After six days of deadlock, the House chose Jefferson. To avoid this situation in the future, the Twelfth Amendment to the Constitution established separate votes for President and Vice President.

Lesson Vocabulary

sedition the act of stirring up rebellion against a government

states' rights the right of states to limit the power of the federal government

nullify to cancel

Lesson Summary
JEFFERSON'S PRESIDENCY

The new President saw his election as a chance to introduce new ideas. He thought of it as the "Revolution of 1800." Jefferson's first goal was to reduce the federal government's power over states and citizens. He believed in an idea known as **laissez faire**, which means that the government should not interfere with the economy.

The *Marbury* v. *Madison* case changed the relationship of the three branches of government. This ruling established **judicial review**, or the authority of the Supreme Court to strike down unconstitutional laws.

In 1801, Jefferson discovered that Spain had secretly transferred New Orleans and the rest of its Louisiana territory to France. Jefferson feared that Napoleon Bonaparte, the French leader, intended to expand France's control in America.

In 1802, before the transfer of Louisiana to France took place, Spain withdrew the right of Americans to ship their goods through New Orleans. Westerners demanded that Jefferson go to war to win back their rights.

Instead, Jefferson sent James Monroe to Paris to offer to buy the city of New Orleans and a territory to the east called West Florida from the French. Monroe was assisted by Robert Livingston, the American minister in Paris.

Around this time, a revolution had driven the French from their Caribbean colony of Haiti. Without this base, France would have trouble defending Louisiana in a war. At the same time, tensions between France and Britain were rising, and war loomed. Napoleon needed money to support the war effort. As a result, France offered to sell not only New Orleans but the entire Louisiana Territory to the United States. The territory stretched from the Gulf of Mexico to Canada and from the Mississippi River to the Rocky Mountains.

Jefferson was delighted with the deal, which almost doubled the size of the country and gave the United States control of the Mississippi.

Even before the United States had bought Louisiana, Jefferson called on Congress to finance a western **expedition**, or a long and carefully organized journey. Army officers Meriwether Lewis and William Clark were to lead the expedition.

(Continues on the next page.)

Lesson Vocabulary

laissez faire the idea that government should play as small a role as possible in economic affairs

judicial review the power of the Supreme Court to decide whether the acts of a President or laws passed by Congress are constitutional

expedition a long voyage of exploration

TOPIC 5 LESSON 4

Lesson Summary

JEFFERSON'S PRESIDENCY

(Continued from page 59)

Trade with Europe was critical to the U.S. economy. After the American Revolution, pirates began attacking American ships in the Mediterranean Sea. The pirates came from four North African countries known as the Barbary States. They were Morocco, Algiers, Tunisia, and Tripoli. European nations paid the Barbary States **tribute**, or money paid by one country to another in return for protection. In exchange, pirates left their ships alone.

For a time, the United States also paid tribute. But Jefferson put an end to that practice and sent warships to the Mediterranean to protect American merchant ships. At first these military patrols went badly. For example, the warship *Philadelphia* ran aground near the Tripoli coast, and its crew was captured. However, the next year, a small force of American marines marched 600 miles across the Sahara to capture Tripoli. This victory inspired confidence in the ability of the United States to deal forcefully with threats from foreign powers.

By 1803 Britain and France were once again at war. The United States, which remained neutral, continued trading with both countries. Britain and France began seizing American ships carrying trade goods to the other country. This was an attempt to weaken each other by cutting off the other's foreign trade. In addition, Britain impressed, or forced, thousands of American sailors to serve in the British navy.

Jefferson tried to force Britain and France to respect American neutrality by issuing an **embargo**. This is a government order that forbids foreign trade. In 1807, Congress passed the Embargo Act. The embargo applied to American ships sailing to any foreign port. Jefferson predicted that France and Britain would soon stop attacking American ships.

However, Jefferson did not foresee the result of the embargo. The big loser proved to be the American economy.

Lesson Vocabulary

tribute a payment by a weaker party to a stronger party in return for protection

embargo a ban on trade

Name_____ Class_____ Date_____

Lesson Summary
MADISON AND THE WAR OF 1812

When James Madison became President in 1809, Americans were angry with the British for supplying arms to Native Americans and impressing American sailors. To most Americans, the country's honor was at stake. They felt a new sense of **nationalism**, or pride in one's country.

After the Battle of Fallen Timbers, tens of thousands of settlers moved westward. Ohio became a state in 1803, and settlers moved into Indiana Territory and beyond.

The tide of settlement had a terrible impact on Native Americans. Westward expansion exposed Native Americans to disease, threatened their hunting grounds, and drove away game. The Native American population declined, as did the power of their traditional leaders.

Two Shawnee brothers, the warrior Tecumseh and the prophet Tenskwatawa, began urging Native American resistance. They called on Native Americans to preserve their traditional ways.

American officials were concerned by Tecumseh's activities. While Tecumseh was gone, William Henry Harrison, the governor of the Indiana Territory, led an attack on Shawnee villages on the Tippecanoe River. Harrison's troops defeated the Native Americans. The Battle of Tippecanoe marked the high point of Native American resistance to settlement. Still, Tecumseh and his warriors continued their struggle for several more years.

In 1810, Henry Clay of Kentucky and John C. Calhoun of South Carolina became leaders in the House of Representatives. The two men and their supporters were called **War Hawks** because they were eager for war with Britain. Opposition to war was strongest in New England, where many believed war would harm American trade.

Relations with Britain worsened in the spring of 1812 when the British told the United States they would continue impressing sailors. Meanwhile, Native Americans in the Northwest began new attacks on frontier settlements. In June, Congress declared war on Britain.

Britain was still at war in Europe at the time, but it was not willing to meet American demands in order to avoid war. When the war began, Americans were confident they would win. However, because of military cuts under Jefferson, the United States military was not prepared for war.

(Continues on the next page.)

Lesson Vocabulary

nationalism a devotion to one's nation and its interests

War Hawks the members of Congress from the South and the West who called for war with Britain prior to the War of 1812

Name_____ Class_____ Date_____

MODIFIED CORNELL NOTES

(Continued from page 61)

At the beginning of the war, Britain set up a blockade of the American coast. A blockade is the action of shutting a port or road to prevent people or supplies from coming into an area or leaving it. By the end of the war, the British were able to close off all American ports.

One early naval success for the United States was the USS *Constitution*'s defeat of the British warship *Guerrière*.

In the West, the Americans and British fought for control of the Great Lakes and the Mississippi River. The British captured American General William Hull's troops after they tried to invade Canada. American forces under Oliver Hazard Perry, however, scored an important victory against the British on Lake Erie. William Henry Harrison and his troops defeated the British at the Battle of the Thames. In the South, Creek warriors attacked several American settlements. Andrew Jackson led American troops to victory against the Creeks in the Battle of Horseshoe Bend.

After the British defeated Napoleon in 1814, they sent more troops to fight against the United States. In August, British troops attacked Washington, D.C., burning several government buildings, including the White House. The British moved on to Baltimore, where they attacked Fort McHenry. British warships bombarded the fort throughout the night of September 13, 1814. At dawn, however, the Americans still held the fort. An American, Francis Scott Key, witnessed the battle and wrote the poem, "The Star-Spangled Banner." Set to music, it later became the national anthem of the United States.

Britain began to tire of war, so the two sides began negotiating a peace treaty. On Christmas Eve 1814, the United States and Britain signed the Treaty of Ghent, ending the war. It took several weeks for the news to reach the United States, and during this time, the two sides fought one last battle. In January 1815, American forces under General Andrew Jackson defeated the British at the Battle of New Orleans.

Meanwhile, opponents of the war met in Hartford, Connecticut, in December 1814. Some delegates suggested that New England secede, or withdraw, from the United States. However, the convention quickly ended when news of the treaty arrived.

To some Americans, the War of 1812 was the "Second War of Independence." Once and for all, the United States had secured its independence from Britain, and European nations would now have to treat the young republic with respect.

Lesson Summary
MONROE'S PRESIDENCY

MODIFIED CORNELL NOTES

After the War of 1812, the Republicans controlled the government. Republican James Monroe's huge victory in the 1816 presidential election crushed the Federalist Party. To promote national unity, Monroe toured parts of the country. He was warmly greeted even in states that had not voted for him in 1816. A Boston newspaper called the new spirit of national unity the "Era of Good Feelings," and the name has been used to describe Monroe's two terms as President.

After 1815, three gifted members of Congress emerged. Henry Clay of Kentucky represented the West. John C. Calhoun of South Carolina spoke for southern interests. Daniel Webster of Massachusetts was a leading politician for the Northeast.

After the War of 1812, British companies began to sell manufactured goods below market price in America, a practice known as dumping. This drove many New England companies out of business. Congress responded by passing the Tariff of 1816, which taxed foreign goods like cloth, iron, leather goods, and paper. Congress passed even higher tariffs in 1818 and 1824. Such protective tariffs were popular in the North, where they protected local factories. But in the South, people resented the high tariffs that made goods more expensive.

Henry Clay defended high tariffs in a plan he called the American System. He said the money from tariffs could pay to build infrastructure, such as bridges, canals, and roads. Clay argued that this would help all regions. Southerners rejected the American System and continued to oppose the tariffs.

(Continues on the next page.)

TOPIC
5
LESSON 6

Lesson Summary
MONROE'S PRESIDENCY

MODIFIED CORNELL NOTES

(Continued from page 63)

Between 1819 and 1824, the Supreme Court issued three major rulings that affected the economy and the power of the federal government. In *Dartmouth College* v. *Woodward* (1819), the Court protected private contracts. A **contract** is an agreement between two or more parties that can be enforced by law. This ruling promoted **capitalism**, an economic system in which private businesses compete in a free market. In *McCulloch* v. *Maryland* (1819), the Court ruled that a state cannot pass a law that violates a federal law. In addition, the Court said states had no power to interfere with federal institutions. This protected the Second Bank of the United States from being taxed by the state of Maryland. In *Gibbons* v. *Ogden* (1824), the Court blocked New York State from giving a steamboat company the sole right to carry passengers on the Hudson River. Because the trip involved trade between two or more states, it was considered **interstate commerce**. Only Congress can regulate such trade. The *McCulloch* v. *Maryland* and *Gibbons* v. *Ogden* rulings both increased the power of the federal government when dealing with the states.

Spain's control of its American colonies was also fading. The people of Latin America were inspired by the American and French revolutions to seek independence. In 1810, Father Miguel Hidalgo (ee *DAHL* goh) led an unsuccessful rebellion against Spanish rule in Mexico. But in 1820, there was another revolution, forcing Spain to grant Mexico independence in 1821. Mexico overthrew its emperor and became a republic in 1823.

In South America, Simón Bolívar (see *MOHN* boh *LEE* vahr) led several struggles for independence. By 1825, most of Latin America had thrown off European rule.

Spain also realized that it could not defend Florida from the United States, so it decided to give up the territory. Spain ceded, or gave up, Florida to the United States in the Adams-Onís Treaty of 1819.

(Continues on the next page.)

Lesson Vocabulary

contract an agreement between two or more parties that can be enforced by law

capitalism an economic system in which private businesses compete in a free market

interstate commerce business that crosses state lines

Lesson Summary
MONROE'S PRESIDENCY

(Continued from page 64)

MODIFIED CORNELL NOTES

In a message to Congress in 1823, the President stated what is now called the Monroe Doctrine. The United States would not allow European nations to create American colonies or to interfere with the free nations of Latin America. Any attempt to do so would be considered "dangerous to our peace and safety." In truth, the United States was not strong enough to block European action. Only the British navy could do that. As U.S. power grew, however, the Monroe Doctrine boosted the influence of the United States in the region.

TOPIC 5 — Review Questions
THE EARLY REPUBLIC

Answer the questions below using the information in the Lesson Summaries on the previous pages.

Lesson 1: Washington's Presidency

1. **Summarize** What two crises occurred during the early part of President Washington's administration, and how were they resolved?

   _____

   _____

2. What were the three parts to Hamilton's financial plan?

   _____

   _____

Lesson 2: The Origin of Political Parties

3. Why did the Framers of the Constitution not expect political parties to develop?

   _____

   _____

4. **Contrast** What were the two political parties' positions on the power of the national government?

   _____

   _____

Lesson 3: John Adams's Presidency

5. What was President Adams's response to problems with France after the XYZ Affair?

   _____

   _____

6. **Identify Central Ideas** What two principles did the Virginia and Kentucky resolutions help establish?

   _____

   _____

TOPIC 5

Review Questions (continued)

THE EARLY REPUBLIC

Lesson 4: Jefferson's Presidency

7. How did the *Marbury* v. *Madison* case change the relationship of the three branches of government?

_____

_____

8. Identify Cause and Effect What were the immediate effects of the Louisiana Purchase?

_____

_____

Lesson 5: Madison and the War of 1812

9. What British actions led to the War of 1812?

_____

_____

10. Define What was the Treaty of Ghent?

_____

_____

Lesson 6: Monroe's Presidency

11. Why did Congress pass protective tariffs?

_____

_____

12. Analyze Information How did the Supreme Court's rulings increase the power of the federal government?

_____

_____

Name_____ Class_____ Date_____

Focus Question: In the years from 1820 to 1860, the United States grew to stretch "from sea to shining sea." What were some key developments that made this growth possible? What problems resulted from this rapid and massive expansion?

As you read, note specific examples of key developments from 1820 to 1860 that made the nation's growth possible and of problems that the expansion caused.

	Developments Making Growth Possible	Problems Created by Expansion
Westward Growth of the Nation	•	•

Name_____ Class_____ Date_____

By 1824, **suffrage**—the right to vote—had been granted to almost all adult white males, not just those who owned property. However, suffrage was still restricted. Women and enslaved African Americans could not participate in government. States also were changing how they chose presidential electors. Previously, state legislatures chose them. Now, that right went to the voters. In 1824, the voters in 18 out of 24 states chose their electors.

Greater voting rights were part of a larger spread of democratic ideas. Jackson and his supporters believed that ordinary people should vote and hold public office. Jackson did not trust government and banks, which he felt favored the rich. Jackson and his supporters strongly opposed special privileges for those of high social status.

Adams pushed for a program of economic growth through internal improvements. He called for the government to pay for the construction of new roads and canals. He also favored projects promoting the arts and sciences.

Democratic-Republicans who supported Adams called themselves the National Republicans. In 1834, many of them joined a new party, known as the Whig Party. Whigs had their highest level of support in the Northeast because their policies aimed to help manufacturing and commerce. Jackson and other Democratic-Republicans began to call themselves the Democratic Party. Democrats had support in the South and West because their policies supported farmers and workers.

In the presidential election of 1824, Jackson won the most popular and electoral votes, but not a majority. According to the Constitution, the House of Representatives would have to decide the election. Candidate and Speaker of the House Henry Clay told his supporters to vote for John Quincy Adams. When Adams was elected and made Clay his Secretary of State, Jackson was outraged. His supporters claimed that Clay and Adams had made a "corrupt bargain." These rumors **burdened** Adams as President. He had ambitious plans for the nation, but he lacked the political skill to push his programs through Congress. Adams never won Americans' trust, and as a result, he served only one term.

(Continues on the next page.)

Lesson Vocabulary

suffrage the right to vote
burdened weighed heavy upon; worried

TOPIC 6 LESSON 1

Lesson Summary
JACKSON WINS THE PRESIDENCY

MODIFIED CORNELL NOTES

(Continued from page 69)

Three times as many people voted in the election of 1828 as had voted in 1824. Most of these new voters supported Jackson, who easily defeated Adams. The election revealed growing sectional and class divisions among voters. Jackson did best in the West and South and had strong support from farmers, small business owners, and workers nationwide. Adams was most popular in his home region of New England.

Jackson's supporters called the election a victory for the "common man." Some supporters called Jackson the "People's President." Tens of thousands of ordinary people came to the Capitol to attend Jackson's inauguration. Once in office, Jackson replaced some government officials with his own supporters. Although this was not a new practice, Jackson openly defended what he was doing. He claimed that bringing in new people furthered democracy. This practice of rewarding supporters of the party that wins an election with government jobs became known as the **spoils system**.

Lesson Vocabulary
spoils system the practice of giving supporters government jobs

TOPIC 6
LESSON 2

Lesson Summary
POLITICAL CONFLICT AND ECONOMIC CRISIS

The issue of states' rights was raised again in 1828 when Congress passed a new **tariff** on manufactured goods. This tariff helped northern businesses but hurt southerners, who were forced to pay more for goods. Southerners felt the law was unfair, and to many, the tariff issue was part of a larger problem. If the federal government could enforce what southerners considered an unjust law, could it also use its power to ban slavery? Vice President John C. Calhoun argued that the states had the right of **nullification**—an action by a state that cancels a federal law to which the state objects.

When Congress passed another high tariff in 1832, South Carolina voted to nullify the tariffs. State leaders also threatened to secede, or leave, the Union. Jackson asked Congress to allow the federal government to collect its tariff by force if necessary. But he also supported a compromise bill that would lower the tariffs. In 1832, Congress passed both laws. South Carolina accepted the new tariff, ending the crisis.

The second Bank of the United States earned strong support from business people. The Bank loaned money to many businesses and was a safe place for the federal government to keep its money. The money it issued formed a stable currency. But Andrew Jackson and many other Americans believed that the Bank favored the rich and hurt everyday people. For example, the Bank sometimes limited the amount of money that state banks could lend. In the South and West, the Bank was blamed for the economic crisis of 1819, which cost many people their farms.

In 1832, Nicholas Biddle, the Bank's president, got Congress to renew the Bank's charter. Jackson vetoed this bill, promising to defeat Biddle. Most voters stood behind Jackson, who won the election by a large margin. As a result, the Bank ceased to exist when its charter ran out in 1836.

Since the founding of the United States, Americans have debated how to divide power between the federal government and the states. The Constitution gives the federal government many significant powers, but at the same time, the Tenth Amendment states that powers not specifically given to the federal government are reserved to the states or to the people. Over the years, the issue of balancing federal and state power has come up repeatedly. During Jackson's presidency, arguments over this issue caused a serious crisis.

(Continues on the next page.)

Lesson Vocabulary

tariff tax on goods coming into a country

nullification the idea that a state has the right to nullify, or cancel, a federal law that the state leaders consider to be unconstitutional

Lesson Summary
POLITICAL CONFLICT AND ECONOMIC CRISIS

MODIFIED CORNELL NOTES

(Continued from page 71)

Martin Van Buren, Jackson's Vice President, won the presidency in 1836. Just as he took office, the U.S. economy faced the Panic of 1837. British mills began buying less cotton, which caused cotton prices to fall. Cotton growers could not repay their bank loans, which caused hundreds of banks to fail. Van Buren's presidency was ruined.

In 1840, the Whig candidate, William Henry Harrison, easily beat Van Buren. The Age of Jackson had ended.

Name_____ Class_____ Date_____

Lesson Summary
NATIVE AMERICANS ON THE FRONTIER

In 1828, more than 100,000 Native Americans lived east of the Mississippi River. These nations included the Cherokee, Chickasaw, Choctaw, and Creek. The groups lived in various parts of Alabama, Mississippi, Georgia, North Carolina, and Tennessee. The Seminoles, who lived in Florida, had an unusual origin. They were a combination of Creeks who had moved into Florida in the late 1700s, Florida Native Americans, and escaped African American slaves. Many of the southeastern Native Americans were farmers or lived in towns.

The Cherokees, in particular, adopted some white customs. Many Cherokees became Christians. They also had businesses, small industries, schools, and even a newspaper written in English and Cherokee. The alphabet for the Cherokee language was created by a leader named Sequoyah (sih KWOY uh). In 1827, the Cherokee set up a government based on a written constitution. They claimed status as a separate nation.

To many government leaders and white farmers, Native Americans stood in the way of westward expansion. Furthermore, Native Americans lived on **fertile** land. White farmers wanted that land for growing cotton.

Policies to move Native Americans from their lands dated from the presidency of Thomas Jefferson. Jefferson thought that the only way to prevent conflict and protect Native American culture was to send the Native Americans west. After the War of 1812, the federal government signed treaties with several Native American groups in the Old Northwest. Groups agreed to give up their land and move west of the Mississippi River. The pressure to move increased on the Native Americans who remained in the Southeast.

(Continues on the next page.)

Lesson Vocabulary
fertile good for growing

TOPIC 6 LESSON 3

Lesson Summary

NATIVE AMERICANS ON THE FRONTIER

(Continued from page 73)

MODIFIED CORNELL NOTES

In 1825 and 1827, the state of Georgia passed a law that forced the Creeks to give up most of their land. Then, in 1828, Georgia tried to get the Cherokees to leave the state, but they refused to move, choosing instead to sue the state of Georgia. Two cases eventually made their way to the Supreme Court. The first case, *Cherokee Nation* v. *Georgia*, reached the Supreme Court in 1831. The decision in this suit went against the Cherokees. However, in the second case, *Worcester* v. *Georgia* (1832), the Court declared that Georgia's laws "can have no force" within Cherokee land. In his ruling, John Marshall pointed to treaties that the United States had signed guaranteeing certain territory to Native Americans. These treaties meant Georgia could not take away Cherokee territory. President Andrew Jackson, who wanted to move Native Americans to the West, refused to support the Court's decision. Instead, Jackson chose to enforce the Indian Removal Act of 1830. This law gave him the power to offer Native Americans land west of the Mississippi for their land in the East.

Believing they had no choice, most Native American leaders signed treaties agreeing to move westward to Indian Territory. Today, most of that area is in the state of Oklahoma. The Choctaws signed the first treaty in 1830, and they moved between 1831 and 1833. However, the federal government did not give the Choctaw enough food and supplies for the long trip. As a result, many people died in the cold winter weather. The Cherokees held out a few years longer. Finally, President Martin Van Buren forced the Cherokees to move in the winter of 1838–1839 while being guarded by 7,000 soldiers. Once again, there were not enough supplies. Some 4,000 of the 15,000 Cherokees who began the journey died along the route that became known as the Trail of Tears.

The Seminoles refused to move, choosing instead to fight a war against removal. In the 1840s, most Seminoles were eventually removed to Indian Territory. In their new homes, Native Americans struggled to rebuild their lives under very difficult conditions.

Lesson Vocabulary

sue to bring a case against someone in court

TOPIC

6

LESSON 4

Lesson Summary
WESTWARD MOVEMENT

MODIFIED CORNELL NOTES

As the U.S. population grew, more people moved west to find new land. As more people moved west, better forms of transportation developed.

Settlers began moving west into what is now Ohio and Kentucky as early as the 1700s. In 1775, pioneer Daniel Boone helped create the Wilderness Road, a new route to the West. Others traveled down the Ohio River in **flatboats**, or flat-bottomed boats. By the early 1800s, the flow of immigrants to the West had become a flood. As western populations grew, many areas applied to become states. Between 1792 and 1819, eight states joined the Union: Kentucky (1792), Tennessee (1796), Ohio (1803), Louisiana (1812), Indiana (1816), Mississippi (1817), Illinois (1818), and Alabama (1819).

Traveling west was not easy. Roads were unpaved, rough, and easily washed out by rain. The nation needed better roads. Private companies began building **turnpikes**, or toll roads. One example was the Lancaster Turnpike in Pennsylvania, a road of gravel topped with flat stones that provided a smooth ride. In marshy areas, builders constructed **corduroy roads** out of sawed-off logs laid side by side. These roads were bumpy and noisy. The first road built with federal money was the National Road. Begun in 1811 in Cumberland, Maryland, the road eventually stretched to Illinois.

The invention of the steam engine changed travel. Robert Fulton's successful steamboat, the *Clermont*, ushered in the age of steamboats in 1807. Steamboats moved passengers and goods throughout the nation quickly and cheaply. Flat-bottomed steamboats could even travel in shallow western rivers. But steamboats were not always safe. They could catch fire or explode.

The fastest, cheapest way to ship goods was by water, but natural waterways did not connect all parts of the nation. The solution was to build canals, or channels that are dug across land and filled with water. Canals allow boats to reach more places. Governor DeWitt Clinton of New York suggested that a canal be built to connect the Hudson River and Lake Erie. Building the canal was challenging for engineers and workers. After the canal was finished in 1825, it allowed people to ship goods for about one tenth of the previous cost. The success of the Erie Canal sparked a surge of canal building and made New York City a commercial hub.

Lesson Vocabulary

flatboat a boat with a flat bottom used for transporting heavy loads on inland waterways

turnpike a road that travelers must pay a toll to use

corduroy road a road made of logs

TOPIC 6
LESSON 5

Lesson Summary
SETTLING OREGON COUNTRY

MODIFIED CORNELL NOTES

Glowing reports of Oregon Country led more easterners to make the journey west. Farmers sought the free and fertile land, the mild climate, and the plentiful rainfall in river valleys. Settlers from all over the country began to come down with "Oregon Fever."

Trade drove the first western crossings. Traders were looking for new markets in which to sell their goods. In the process, they blazed important trails for those who followed.

Beaver fur was in great demand in the East. However, by the 1830s, the supply of beavers was nearly **exhausted**, so most of the trappers moved back east to become farmers, merchants, or even bankers. Others stayed as guides for the wagon trains that brought thousands of settlers west in the 1840s.

Most settlers followed the Oregon Trail, a route that stretched over 2,000 miles from Missouri to Oregon. Travelers left in the spring and had five months to make their journey. If they were caught in the Rocky Mountains during the winter, their chances of survival were slim.

Pioneers on the Oregon Trail banded together in wagon trains for mutual protection. During the day, teams of horses or oxen would pull the long trains of covered wagons, which were filled with the settlers' food and possessions. Meanwhile, the pioneers would walk, often for 15 hours a day. At night, the wagons were drawn up in a circle to keep the cattle from wandering off. The trip was a great hardship and very dangerous.

Lesson Vocabulary
glowing praising highly
exhausted consumed or used up

Name_____ Class_____ Date_____

In 1820, the Spanish gave Moses Austin a land grant to establish a small colony in Texas. After Moses Austin died, his son, Stephen Austin, led a group of some 300 settlers there. After Mexico won its independence from Spain and took possession of Texas, Texans came into conflict with the Mexican government. Mexico had outlawed slavery, but settlers brought slaves in. Texans wanted a democratic government.

In 1833, General Antonio López de Santa Anna became president of Mexico. He overturned Mexico's democratic constitution and became a **dictator**, or person with absolute power. Texans, including Tejanos of Mexican descent, decided to resist Santa Anna's power over Texas. A war for independence began with a battle at Gonzales in 1835. The Republic of Texas was created in 1836.

Texan troops under the leadership of Sam Houston faced a difficult struggle to win their independence. Mexican soldiers defeated a small group of Texans at the famous battle at the Alamo after a long **siege** there. The loss inspired the Texans to fight harder. Santa Anna surrendered after the Battle of Jacinto in April 1836.

After Sam Houston defeated Santa Anna, he became president of the Republic of Texas. He had to deal with many problems. Texans hoped the United States would **annex**, or add on, their republic to the Union. Annexation became a major U.S. political issue because Texas would come in as a slave state. Disagreement slowed annexation, but the Republic grew through immigration from both the United States and other nations. In 1845, the United States agreed to annex Texas.

Lesson Vocabulary

dictator a ruler with absolute power and authority over a country, usually through the use of violence

siege to surround and blockade an enemy town or position with troops in order to force it to surrender

annex to take over

MODIFIED CORNELL NOTES

TOPIC 6
LESSON 7

Lesson Summary
MANIFEST DESTINY IN CALIFORNIA AND THE SOUTHWEST

After Mexico won independence, it allowed trade with the United States. In 1821, Captain William Becknell led a wagon train filled with merchandise from Independence, Missouri, to Santa Fe, New Mexico. It was a difficult journey, but Becknell's group reached Santa Fe. The Santa Fe Trail soon became a busy international trade route.

Spanish missionaries tried to convert the local American Indians to Catholicism. Many American Indians were forced to live and work at missions. In the end, thousands of American Indians died from overwork or disease.

Spain also removed the missions from church control and gave their lands in large **land grants**, or government gifts of land, to Mexican settlers. Many of these grants were made to **rancheros**, or owners of ranches. Much of this land belonged to American Indians, who responded by raiding ranches. However, they were soon crushed, and their population in the Southwest was drastically reduced.

Many Americans were interested in westward **expansion**, or extending the nation beyond its existing borders. Under Jefferson, the Louisiana Purchase had doubled the size of the nation. But just years later, Americans were looking even farther west. A newspaper editor coined the phrase "manifest destiny" in 1845. The phrase described the belief that the United States was destined, or meant, to stretch from coast to coast.

Annexation became a major political issue because Texas would come in as a slave state. How could the balance of slave and free states be maintained? President James K. Polk solved this problem by negotiating a treaty to acquire Oregon from Britain. In 1845, Texas was admitted as a slave state. Oregon was annexed as a free territory.

But trouble was looming. Mexico had never recognized Texas independence. Now Mexico claimed that the southern border of Texas was the Nueces River, not the Rio Grande. Polk pressured Mexico to accept the Rio Grande border.

The United States and Mexico signed the Treaty of Guadalupe-Hidalgo in 1848. Mexico recognized Texas as a U.S. state. Then in the Mexican Cession, it gave present-day California, Nevada, and Utah, as well as parts of Wyoming, Colorado, Arizona, and New Mexico to the United States for $18 million.

(Continues on the next page.)

Lesson Vocabulary

land grant a government gift of land

ranchero owner of a ranch

expansion extending the nation beyond its existing borders

TOPIC 6

LESSON 7

Lesson Summary

MANIFEST DESTINY IN CALIFORNIA AND THE SOUTHWEST

(Continued from page 78)

After the Mexican Cession, easterners began migrating to California. At the time, there were about 10,000 Californios, or Mexican Californians, living in the territory.

A flood of other settlers came to California when gold was discovered in 1848 at Sutter's Mill near Sacramento. News of the discovery spread quickly, and the prospect of finding gold drew about 80,000 fortune seekers. These people who came to California in search of gold were known as the "**forty-niners**." In just two years, California's population zoomed from 14,000 to 100,000. Prospectors, or gold seekers, searched throughout the Sacramento Valley for gold.

The gold rush brought enormous ethnic diversity to California. People came from Europe, Asia, Australia, and South America. After news of the gold rush reached China, about 45,000 Chinese men went to California. They faced prejudice and were generally hired only for menial labor.

Lesson Vocabulary

forty-niner a term to describe one of more than 80,000 people who joined the California Gold Rush in 1849

TOPIC 6 — Review Questions
THE AGE OF JACKSON AND WESTWARD EXPANSION

Answer the questions below using the information in the Lesson Summaries on the previous pages.

Lesson 1: Jackson Wins the Presidency

1. **Contrast** What was different about the voting rights enjoyed by citizens in 1824 compared to earlier elections?

_____

_____

2. What were the origins of and the sources of support for the Whig Party and the Democratic Party?

_____

_____

Lesson 2: Political Conflict and Economic Crisis

3. **Compare Points of View** What did supporters and opponents of the second Bank of the United States believe?

_____

_____

4. What caused the nullification crisis?

_____

_____

Lesson 3: Native Americans on the Frontier

5. What were two reasons government leaders and white farmers wanted to move Native Americans from their land?

_____

_____

6. **Make Generalizations** What happened to most of the Native American groups in the Southeast?

_____

_____

Lesson 4: Westward Movement

7. Why were canals and better roads needed?

_____

_____

TOPIC 6 — Review Questions (continued)
THE AGE OF JACKSON AND WESTWARD EXPANSION

8. Explain How did the invention of the steam engine change travel?

_____

_____

Lesson 5: Settling Oregon Country

9. What features drew eastern farmers to settle in Oregon?

_____

_____

10. Predict Consequences How did traders' search for new markets in the West drive the first western crossings?

_____

_____

Lesson 6: Independence for Texas

11. Why did Texans come into conflict with the Mexican government after it took possession of Texas?

_____

_____

12. Identify Central Issues Why was annexation a major political issue?

_____

_____

Lesson 7: Manifest Destiny in California and the Southwest

13. What belief did the phrase "manifest destiny" describe?

_____

_____

14. Determine Relevance Why were the Treaty of Guadalupe-Hidalgo and the Mexican Cession important to the growth of the United States?

_____

_____

TOPIC 7

Note Taking Study Guide
SOCIETY AND CULTURE BEFORE THE CIVIL WAR

Focus Question: Describe the economy in the South in the decades prior to the Civil War, and explain why southerners in that period resisted efforts to end slavery.

As you read, think about the relationships between events in the late 1700s and early 1800s. Pay particular attention to how these events affected the economy of the Southern United States. Use the flowchart to correctly organize these events. Add more boxes if necessary.

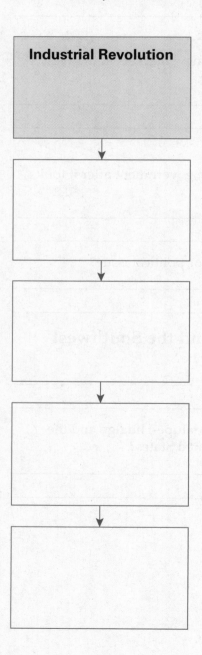

Industrial Revolution

Possible Answers:

- Cotton gin invented, makes cotton processing faster.

- Demand for cheap or slave labor increases.

- Demand for cotton increases.

- Textiles are easier and cheaper to produce.

TOPIC 7 LESSON 1 — Lesson Summary
THE INDUSTRIAL REVOLUTION AND LIFE IN THE NORTH

In the 1700s, machines and new sources of power such as water and steam began to replace labor once performed by people and animals. This Industrial Revolution, as it was called, greatly changed the way people lived and worked.

The Industrial Revolution began in Britain in the textile industry. For centuries, workers had spun thread and woven cloth in their own homes. In the 1760s, the spinning jenny speeded up the thread-making process. Then, Richard Arkwright invented the water frame, a spinning machine powered by running water rather than by human energy. This created a new way of working called the **factory system**, in which workers and machines come together in one place outside the home. Mill owners turned to capitalists for money to build factories and machines. **Capitalists** invest capital, or money, in a business to earn a profit.

Another key innovation in American industry was the invention of **interchangeable parts**—identical pieces that could be quickly put together by unskilled workers. Traditionally, craftsmen had built machines by hand. No two parts were the same, making machinery slow to build and hard to repair. Eli Whitney came up with the idea for interchangeable parts in the 1790s. The idea led to mass production—the rapid manufacture of large numbers of identical objects. As a result, many goods became cheaper, and American industry continued to grow.

Many factories, mines, and mills employed children. These children had little chance for an education and worked in difficult conditions. Working conditions for adults were no better.

(Continues on the next page.)

Lesson Vocabulary

factory system the method of producing goods that brought workers and machinery together in one place

capitalist a person who invests in a business to make a profit

interchangeable parts identical, machine-made parts for a tool or an instrument

TOPIC
7
LESSON 1

Lesson Summary
THE INDUSTRIAL REVOLUTION AND LIFE IN THE NORTH

(Continued from page 83)

In the 1800s, the Industrial Revolution led to **urbanization**, or the growth of cities due to movement of people from rural areas to cities. As capitalists built more factories, agricultural workers were attracted to the new types of work available in the cities. As cities in the East became crowded, newly arrived immigrants headed westward. Growing cities faced many problems. Poor sewers, a lack of clean drinking water, and filthy city streets encouraged the spread of disease. Citywide fires were another major concern. Most city buildings were made of wood. Cities relied on volunteer firefighters who had little training or equipment.

American inventors helped industry grow. In 1844, Samuel F.B. Morse tested the **telegraph**, an invention that used electrical signals to send messages very quickly over long distances. The telegraph revolutionized communication. In the Midwest, Cyrus McCormick built a mechanical reaper that cut wheat much faster than could be done by hand. Such machines allowed more wheat to be grown and harvested using fewer workers. This made it easier for farmers to settle the prairies of the Midwest. Other inventions revolutionized the way goods were made. The invention of the sewing machine made the production of clothing more efficient. Introduced in 1846 by Elias Howe and improved by Isaac Singer, sewing machines could make clothes faster and cheaper than ever before.

In 1850, a new type of American-built ship appeared—the clipper ship. Long and slender with tall masts, clipper ships were the fastest vessels on the ocean. But the Yankee clippers, as they were called, were eventually replaced by faster oceangoing steamships.

Of all the forms of transportation, railroads did the most to tie together raw materials, manufacturers, and markets. In 1830, Peter Cooper built the first American-made steam **locomotive**. By 1840, there were 3,000 miles of railroad track in the United States.

As industrialization progressed, life changed for workers. They worked longer hours for lower wages. Most factories had no safety devices, and accidents were common. There were no laws regulating working conditions or protecting injured workers.

(Continues on the next page.)

Lesson Vocabulary

urbanization the movement of population from farms to cities

telegraph a communications device that sends electrical signals along a wire

locomotive an engine that pulls a railroad train

Lesson Summary
THE INDUSTRIAL REVOLUTION AND LIFE IN THE NORTH

(Continued from page 84)

In the 1840s, millions of immigrants came to the United States, mainly from western Europe. In 1845, disease wiped out the potato crop in Ireland. Because the potato was the staple food for most of the population, Ireland suffered from a **famine**, or widespread starvation. Huge numbers of Irish came to America, most of them former farm laborers. Many took jobs laying railroad track or as household workers. Many Germans also came to the United States, fleeing failed revolutions in Germany. Unlike the Irish, German immigrants came from many levels of society. Most moved to the Midwest.

Some Americans worried about the growing foreign population. These were **nativists**, or people who wanted to preserve the country for white, American-born Protestants.

African Americans in the North also faced **discrimination**, or the denial of equal rights or equal treatment to certain groups of people. Though free, African Americans were often not allowed to vote or to work in factories and skilled trades. Public schools and churches were often segregated. So African Americans formed their own churches. They also started their own newspapers and magazines.

Lesson Vocabulary

famine a severe food shortage

nativist a person opposed to immigration

discrimination a policy or practice that denies equal rights to certain groups of people

TOPIC 7 LESSON 2

Lesson Summary

KING COTTON AND LIFE IN THE SOUTH

As the textile industry in the North grew, the demand for cotton rose. Eli Whitney's invention of the cotton gin in 1793 allowed the South to meet this demand. The cotton gin used a spiked wooden cylinder to remove seeds from cotton fibers.

Cotton became the greatest source of wealth for the United States. The southern "Cotton Kingdom" society was dominated by slaveholding owners of large plantations. Most southern whites accepted the system of slavery. Supporters of slavery said that the system was more humane than the free labor system of the North. But critics pointed out that factory workers could quit a job if conditions became too harsh. Also, critics said people held in slavery often suffered physical or other abuse from white owners. By the 1830s, some northerners were urging that slavery be banned.

The South was dependent on agriculture. It led the nation in livestock production, and farmers grew major cash crops such as cotton, rice, sugar, and tobacco. For this reason, industry remained small and mostly served the farming community. Southern farmers began to depend on the North for industrial goods and also for loans to expand their plantations.

Wealthy families made up a "**cottonocracy**." These families were rich planters who often owned 50 or more enslaved workers. Only 1 in 30 southern farmers belonged to a planter family. Small farmers made up about 75 percent of southern whites and did not own slaves.

Few African Americans in the South were free. Many had purchased their freedom. But laws denied them even basic rights. By law, they were excluded from most jobs. They could not vote, serve on juries, testify against whites in court, or attend public schools. Free African Americans were even discouraged from traveling. They also risked being kidnapped and sold into slavery. Many free African Americans still made valuable contributions to southern life.

However, enslaved African Americans faced greater trials. They had no rights at all. Laws called **slave codes** controlled every aspect of their lives. A Kentucky court ruled in 1828 that ". . . a slave by our code is not treated as a person but as a . . . thing." Most enslaved African Americans did heavy farm labor, but many became skilled workers. Some worked in households. Wherever they worked, they faced the possibility of violent punishment for many offenses.

(Continues on the next page.)

Lesson Vocabulary

"**cottonocracy**" a name for the wealthy planters who made their money from cotton in the mid-1800s

slave codes laws that controlled the lives of enslaved African Americans and denied them basic rights

TOPIC 7 LESSON 2

Lesson Summary

KING COTTON AND LIFE IN THE SOUTH

(Continued from page 86)

(Continued from page 86)

MODIFIED CORNELL NOTES

Enslaved African Americans had only one protection against mistreatment: owners looked on them as valuable property that they needed to keep healthy and productive. Families of enslaved African Americans were often broken apart when slave owners sold one or more of their family members.

After 1808, it was illegal to import enslaved Africans to the United States. Yet African Americans kept many African customs alive, including styles of music and dance. Many looked to the Bible for hope. African Americans composed spirituals—religious folk songs that blended biblical themes with the realities of slavery.

African Americans found ways to resist slavery. Some worked slowly, broke equipment, and even fled to seek freedom in the North. Some led rebellions. Nat Turner led the most famous slave uprising in 1831. He and his companions killed some 60 whites. In reprisal, many innocent African Americans were executed.

TOPIC 7 LESSON 3
Lesson Summary
REFORM MOVEMENTS

In the 1830s, many Americans became interested in **social reform**, or organized attempts to improve conditions of life. Social reform had its roots in both politics and religion. The expansion of democracy during the Age of Jackson helped encourage reform. As the political system became more fair, more people began to support causes such as rights for women and the end of slavery.

Religious ideas were another factor encouraging reform. In the early 1800s, some ministers began questioning traditional views, a movement known as the Second Great Awakening. Leaders of the movement questioned **predestination**, the idea that God decided the fate of a person's soul even before birth. They argued that people's own actions determined their salvation, an idea called the "doctrine of free will." In 1826, the minister Charles Finney held the first of many **revivals**, or huge outdoor religious meetings, to convert sinners and urge people to reform. The Second Great Awakening prompted improvement of self and society.

While utopian reformers attempted to create perfect communities apart from the larger community, others tried to change the existing society. The **temperance movement** was an organized effort to end alcohol abuse and the problems it created. This would be difficult since alcohol was widely used in the United States. Many women were drawn to this movement. Most citizens favored temperance, or moderation in drinking.

Some reformers sought to improve the prison system. Dorothea Dix, a schoolteacher, took up this cause. She supported the building of new, more sanitary, and more humane prisons. She also urged the government to create separate institutions, called asylums, for people with mental illnesses.

Education was another area reformers hoped to change. The Puritans of Massachusetts established the first public schools, or free schools supported by taxes, in 1642. Many reformers believed public schools created better-informed voters and could help immigrants assimilate, or become part of, American culture.

(Continues on the next page.)

Lesson Vocabulary

social reform an organized attempt to improve what is unjust or imperfect in society

predestination the Protestant idea that God decided in advance which people would attain salvation after death

revival a large outdoor religious meeting

temperance movement the campaign against alcohol consumption

TOPIC 7 LESSON 5

Lesson Summary
WOMEN'S RIGHTS

(Continued from page 92)

The Seneca Falls Convention was the birthplace of the women's rights movement. The **women's rights movement** was the organized effort to improve the political, legal, and economic status of women in American society. Stanton and Susan B. Anthony worked closely together. As an unmarried woman, Anthony, a former schoolteacher, abolitionist, and **temperance** supporter, was able to travel to promote their cause. Stanton, who was raising a family, often wrote speeches from home. Together, Stanton and Anthony founded the National Woman Suffrage Association in 1869. They also convinced New York to pass a law protecting women's property rights. Many other states followed, some even revising their laws to allow married women to keep their wages.

Even before Seneca Falls, reformers worked to provide educational opportunities for girls. American schools emphasized education for boys. Girls **seldom** studied advanced subjects like math and science. The women's rights movement focused much attention on education. In 1821, Emma Willard founded the Troy Female Seminary in New York, which served as a model for girls' schools everywhere. Other women also started schools. In 1837, Mary Lyon founded the first college for women, Mount Holyoke Female Seminary.

MODIFIED CORNELL NOTES

Lesson Vocabulary

women's rights movement an organized campaign to win legal, educational, employment, and other rights for women

temperance refraining from alcohol

seldom rarely

TOPIC 7 LESSON 6

Lesson Summary

ARTS AND LITERATURE

MODIFIED CORNELL NOTES

After 1820, artists also began to create a unique American style. They focused on the landscapes around them or on the daily lives of Americans. Painter Thomas Cole was part of the Hudson River School, which was inspired by Romanticism. Artists in this school sought to stir emotion by reproducing the beauty and power of nature.

Herman Melville and Nathaniel Hawthorne changed the optimistic tone of American literature by introducing psychological themes and extreme emotions. Melville's novel *Moby-Dick* (1851) is the story of an obsessed ship captain who destroys himself, his ship, and his crew in pursuit of a whale.

Walt Whitman published *Leaves of Grass* in 1855. Whitman wrote about familiar subjects, but his book of poems shocked many readers because he did not follow the accepted set of rules. Most important, Whitman is seen as the poet who best expressed the democratic American spirit. His poetry celebrated the common man. In his poem "Song of Myself," Whitman reaches out to all people.

Other poets used their poetry for social protest and social reform. John Greenleaf Whittier was a Quaker from Massachusetts. Frances Watkins Harper was an African American woman from Maryland. Both Whittier and Harper wrote poems that described and condemned the evils of slavery.

American music also began to develop its own identity. A wide variety of new songs emerged. The era's most popular songwriter was Stephen Foster. Many of his tunes, such as "Dixie," are still familiar today.

By the early 1800s, a new artistic movement called Romanticism took shape in Europe. It was a style of writing and painting that placed value on nature, emotions or strong feelings, and the imagination. Americans developed their own form of Romanticism, called transcendentalism. Its goal was to explore the relationship between man and nature through emotion rather than through reason.

(Continues on the next page.)

(Continued from page 94)

MODIFIED CORNELL NOTES

   Transcendentalists tried to live simply and sought an understanding of beauty, goodness, and truth. The writings and lectures of Ralph Waldo Emerson reflected transcendentalism. Emerson stressed **individualism**, or the unique importance of the individual. He influenced Henry David Thoreau, another important writer and thinker. In his 1854 book *Walden*, Thoreau urged people to live simply. He also encouraged **civil disobedience**, the idea that people should disobey unjust laws if their consciences demand it.

Lesson Vocabulary

transcendentalist one of a group of New England writers and thinkers who believed that the most important truths transcended, or went beyond, human reason

individualism the belief in the uniqueness and importance of each individual

civil disobedience the act of disobeying laws considered to be unjust as a way of resisting those laws, or a strategy based on such acts

Name_____ Class_____ Date_____

TOPIC 7

Review Questions
SOCIETY AND CULTURE BEFORE THE CIVIL WAR

Answer the questions below using the information in the Lesson Summaries on the previous pages.

Lesson 1: The Industrial Revolution and Life in the North

1. **Describe** How did the Industrial Revolution change working life?

_____

_____

2. How did the Industrial Revolution lead to urbanization, and what problems resulted from the growth of cities?

_____

_____

Lesson 2: King Cotton and Life in the South

3. **Connect** How were cotton and slavery connected?

_____

_____

4. In what ways did free African Americans in the South have their rights taken away?

_____

_____

Lesson 3: Reform Movements

5. What religious movement contributed to reform?

_____

_____

6. **List** What types of social reform were parts of the reform movement?

_____

_____

Lesson 4: Abolitionism

7. **Define** What was the Underground Railroad?

_____

_____

8. How did abolitionists try to end slavery?

_____

_____

TOPIC 7

Review Questions (continued)

SOCIETY AND CULTURE BEFORE THE CIVIL WAR

Lesson 5: Women's Rights

9. In what ways were women's civil and legal rights limited in 1820?

_____

_____

10. Hypothesize Why do you think Elizabeth Cady Stanton based her Declaration of Sentiments on the Declaration of Independence?

_____

_____

Lesson 6: Arts and Literature

11. Make Generalizations How did Herman Melville and Nathaniel Hawthorne change the tone of American literature?

_____

_____

12. Summarize What ideas did the transcendentalist writers express?

_____

_____

Name_____ Class_____ Date_____

Focus Question: In the early 1800s, the North and South developed different economies and social institutions. One key difference was the presence or absence of slavery. How did the two sections address the issue of slavery before, during, and after the Civil War?

As you read the Lesson Summaries on the following pages, note specific ways in which the North and the South addressed the issue of slavery before and during the Civil War.

	North	South
Before the Civil War	•	•
During the Civil War	•	•

TOPIC 8 LESSON 1

Lesson Summary
CONFLICTS AND COMPROMISES

Between 1820 and 1848, the balance between free and slave states was maintained. However, the Missouri Compromise did not apply to the huge territory gained from Mexico in 1848. This compromise had banned slavery north of latitude 36°30′N. Would this new territory be organized as states that allowed slavery?

The issue was important to northerners who wanted to stop slavery from spreading. Fearing that the South would gain too much power, Representative David Wilmot of Pennsylvania proposed in 1846 that Congress ban slavery in all southwestern lands that might become states. This was called the Wilmot Proviso. The proviso passed in the House but not the Senate. Slaveholding states saw it as a northern attack on slavery.

The Democratic presidential candidate in 1848 was Senator Lewis Cass of Michigan. He came up with a slavery plan he thought would work in both the North and South. His idea was to let people in each new territory that applied for statehood decide for themselves whether to allow slavery. This **popular sovereignty** meant that people in each territory would vote directly on the issue, rather than having their elected representatives decide for them.

Many antislavery Whigs and Democrats wanted to take a stronger stand. They created their own party, called the Free-Soil Party. They wanted to ban slavery in all territory gained in the Mexican-American War—making it "free soil."

Both sides realized that California's entrance into the Union would upset the balance of free and slave states. Southerners feared that if free states gained the majority in the Senate, the South could no longer block antislavery proposals. Southern leaders threatened to **secede**, or withdraw, from the Union if California was admitted as a free state.

In 1850, Congress passed and President Millard Fillmore signed a series of five bills based on Henry Clay's proposals that were collectively known as the Compromise of 1850. To please the North, California was admitted as a free state and the slave trade was banned in the nation's capital. To please the South, popular sovereignty would be used to decide the slavery issue in the rest of the Mexican Cession. Southerners also got a tough fugitive slave law.

(Continues on the next page.)

Lesson Vocabulary

popular sovereignty a term used in the mid-1800s to refer to the idea that each territory could decide for itself whether or not to allow slavery

secede to withdraw from membership in a group

TOPIC 8 LESSON 1

Lesson Summary
CONFLICTS AND COMPROMISES

(Continued from page 99)

MODIFIED CORNELL NOTES

The Fugitive Slave Act of 1850 allowed government officials to arrest any person accused of being a runaway slave. Suspects had no right to prove they had been falsely accused in a trial. All that was needed to deprive someone of his or her freedom was the word of one white person. In addition, northerners were required to help capture runaway slaves if authorities requested assistance.

Harriet Beecher Stowe was a northerner committed to fighting slavery. In 1852, she published *Uncle Tom's Cabin*, a book about a kind slave who is abused by a cruel master. The book was a bestseller in the North. It shocked thousands of people who were previously unconcerned about slavery. Stowe's book showed that slavery was not just a political conflict, but a real human problem.

TOPIC 8 LESSON 2

Lesson Summary
GROWING TENSIONS

In 1853, Illinois Senator Stephen A. Douglas suggested forming two new territories—the Kansas Territory and the Nebraska Territory. Southerners objected because both territories lay in an area closed to slavery by the Missouri Compromise. This meant that the states created from these territories would enter the Union as free states.

To win southern support, Douglas proposed that slavery in the new territories be decided by popular sovereignty. In effect, this undid the Missouri Compromise. Northerners were angered that the slavery issue was to be reopened in the territories. Southerners, however, supported Douglas's proposal, which enabled the Kansas-Nebraska Act to pass in both houses of Congress in 1854.

In March 1855, Kansas held a vote on whether to enter the Union as a free or slave state. Thousands of proslavery people from Missouri voted illegally. Kansas had only 3,000 voters, but 8,000 votes were cast. A proslavery government was elected. Antislavery Kansans refused to accept these results and put a second government in place.

Violence soon broke out. Pro- and antislavery groups **terrorized** the countryside, attacking and killing settlers. It was so bad that the territory earned the name Bleeding Kansas.

Violence even spilled onto the floor of the U.S. Senate. After Massachusetts Senator Charles Sumner attacked a South Carolina senator in a fiery speech, the senator's nephew physically attacked Sumner in the Senate chamber. Many southerners felt that Sumner got what he deserved. To northerners, however, it was further evidence that slavery was brutal and inhumane.

In 1857, the Supreme Court delivered a blow to antislavery forces. It decided the case of *Dred Scott* v. *Sandford*. Dred Scott was an enslaved person who sued for his freedom because he had lived with his master in states where slavery was illegal.

Supreme Court Chief Justice Roger B. Taney ruled that Scott had no right to sue in federal court because African Americans were not citizens. Taney also declared that living in a free state did not make enslaved people free. They were property, and the property rights of their owners were protected in all states.

This meant that Congress did not have the power to prohibit slavery in any territory and that the Missouri Compromise was unconstitutional. Slavery was legal again in all territories. Supporters of slavery rejoiced at this ruling. Northerners, however, were stunned.

(Continues on the next page.)

Lesson Vocabulary
terrorize to inspire fear or terror

TOPIC 8 LESSON 2

Lesson Summary
GROWING TENSIONS

(Continued from page 101)

The Whig Party split apart in 1854 when Whigs who were willing to take a strong antislavery stand joined the new Republican Party. Its main platform was to keep slavery from spreading to the western territories.

Joined by northern Democrats and Free-Soilers, the Republican Party quickly became powerful. It won 105 of 245 seats in the House in the election of 1854. In 1856, John C. Frémont was the first Republican candidate for President. Although Frémont won 11 of the 16 free states, the Democratic candidate, James Buchanan, was elected President.

Abraham Lincoln, an Illinois attorney, was elected to the House as a Whig, where he voted for the Wilmot Proviso. After one term, he returned to his Springfield law practice.

Lincoln's opposition to the Kansas-Nebraska Act brought him back into politics. In 1858, Lincoln ran for the Illinois Senate seat against Stephen Douglas, the author of the Kansas-Nebraska Act. When Lincoln accepted the Republican nomination, he made a stirring speech in favor of the Union. He said the country could not survive "half slave and half free."

Many southerners believed that Lincoln was an abolitionist. Lincoln then challenged Douglas to a series of public debates, and thousands gathered to hear them speak.

John Brown was an abolitionist who had been driven out of Kansas after the Pottawatomie Massacre. He returned to New England and hatched a plot to raise an army to free people in the South who were enslaved. In 1859, Brown and a small band of supporters attacked Harpers Ferry, Virginia. His goal was to seize the arsenal, or gun warehouse, the United States Army had there. He would give the arms to enslaved African Americans and lead them in a revolt.

Brown and his men were captured. Brown was executed, but his cause was celebrated in the North, where many considered him to be a hero. More than ever, southerners were convinced that the North was out to destroy their way of life.

Lesson Vocabulary
arsenal a place where guns are stored

Name_____ Class_____ Date_____

MODIFIED CORNELL NOTES

As the election of 1860 drew near, Americans everywhere felt a sense of crisis. The long and bitter debate over slavery had left the nation seriously divided. Southern Democrats wanted the party to support slavery in the territories. But northerners refused to do so, and the party split in two.

Northern Democrats nominated Stephen Douglas. But southern Democrats picked Vice President John Breckenridge from Kentucky. Some southerners still hoped to heal the split between the North and the South. They formed the Constitutional Union Party and nominated John Bell of Tennessee, who promised to protect slavery *and* keep the nation together. The Republicans chose Abraham Lincoln as their candidate. His criticisms of slavery during his debates with Stephen Douglas made him popular in the North.

To many southerners, Lincoln's election meant that the South no longer had a voice in the national government. They believed that the President and Congress were set against their interests. South Carolina was the first southern state to secede from the Union. Six more states followed.

Not all southerners favored secession. But they were overwhelmed by those who did. By February 1861, leaders from the seven seceding states had met in Montgomery, Alabama, and formed a new nation they called the Confederate States of America. By the time Lincoln took office in March, the Confederate leaders had written a constitution and named former Mississippi Senator Jefferson Davis as their president.

In Lincoln's inaugural address, he assured the seceding states that he meant them no harm. He stated that he had no plan to abolish slavery where it already existed. Lincoln's assurance of friendship was rejected. The seceding states took over post offices, forts, and other federal property within their borders.

One of those forts was Fort Sumter, which was on an island in the harbor of Charleston, South Carolina. The fort's commander would not surrender. South Carolina authorities decided to starve the fort's troops into surrender. They had been cut off from supplies since late December and could not hold out much longer.

Lincoln did not want to give up the fort, but he feared that sending troops might cause other states to secede. He decided to send food to the fort, but on supply ships carrying no troops or guns. Confederate leaders decided to capture the fort while it was still cut off from supplies. On April 12, they opened fire. After 34 hours, with the fort on fire, the troops inside finally surrendered. This attack marked the beginning of the American Civil War.

(Continues on the next page.)

TOPIC 8 LESSON 3

Lesson Summary
DIVISION AND THE OUTBREAK OF WAR

MODIFIED CORNELL NOTES

(Continued from page 103)

After Fort Sumter was captured, President Lincoln declared that a rebellion existed in the South. He requested troops to subdue the Confederacy. Some states supplied more than enough volunteers, some refused to comply, and some did not respond. More southern states seceded.

There were four **border states**—slave states that did not secede. These were Delaware, Kentucky, Missouri, and Maryland. Delaware supported the Union. Kentucky started out neutral, not favoring either side, but it supported the Union after it was invaded by southern forces in September 1861.

Most people in Maryland and Missouri favored the South. Lincoln sent troops to occupy Missouri. If Maryland seceded, the U.S. capital would be in Confederate territory, so eastern Maryland was put under **martial law**. This is a type of rule in which the military is in charge and citizens' rights are suspended.

When the war began, people on both sides were confident of victory. To win the war, the North had to invade the South. Southerners would be fighting on their own territory, and they would be led by some of the nation's best officers. The North also had some advantages. It had a larger population, more farmland, and more factories.

Both Lincoln and Davis were strong leaders. While some northerners doubted Lincoln's leadership ability before the war, he proved to be both patient and a fine war planner. Davis was respected for his honesty and courage.

Lesson Vocabulary

border state a slave state that remained in the Union during the Civil War

martial law rule by the military instead of an elected government

Name_____ Class_____ Date_____

TOPIC 8 LESSON 4

Lesson Summary

THE COURSE OF WAR

MODIFIED CORNELL NOTES

To isolate the South, the North set up a naval **blockade**, a military action to prevent traffic to and from an area. If the South could not sell cotton to Britain, it would run out of money to fight. The North planned to control the Mississippi River and seize Richmond, Virginia, the Confederate capital.

Southerners had a simple strategy: defend their land until northerners gave up. They would finance the war with continued trade with Britain. They also hoped Britain would support the South.

The Confederacy used **ironclads** against the Union's naval blockade, and the Union used them in their efforts to control the Mississippi River.

Northerners wanted to end the war quickly with a decisive battle. Popular demand led Union General Irvin McDowell to march into Virginia before his troops were fully trained. The First Battle of Bull Run was fought along Bull Run, a river near Manassas, Virginia, on July 21, 1861. The South held firm, and the poorly trained Union troops panicked and retreated.

After its demoralizing defeat at Bull Run, the Union army got a new commander, General George McClellan. He was an excellent organizer, but he was also a very cautious leader. He spent seven months training his army instead of attacking the Confederate enemy. In March 1862, he finally moved one hundred thousand soldiers by boat to a point southeast of Richmond. He knew that his troops could easily have defeated the 15,000 Confederate soldiers facing them, but the cautious McClellan stopped to ask Lincoln to send him more men. Almost a month passed before he resumed the march.

This delay gave the Confederates plenty of time to reinforce their small army. They stopped McClellan's advancing forces outside Richmond on May 31, 1862, then forced the Union army to retreat in late June.

General Robert E. Lee decided to invade the North, reasoning that a victory on Union soil would win European support for the Confederacy. He moved his army into western Maryland.

When McClellan learned that Lee had divided his army, he attacked the larger half at Antietam Creek near Sharpsburg, Maryland, on September 17, 1862. It was the bloodiest day of the Civil War.

(Continues on the next page.)

Lesson Vocabulary

blockade a group of ships or other military forces arranged to prevent traffic to and from an area

ironclad a ship covered with iron

Lesson Summary

THE COURSE OF WAR

MODIFIED CORNELL NOTES

(Continued from page 105)

The Union army had a new commander in 1862, General Ambrose Burnside, who was determined to act more boldly than General McClellan had. Burnside marched toward Richmond in December 1862 to attack Confederate General Lee's army. Burnside ordered traditional charges, sending thousands of men running into Confederate gunfire. The Union lost 13,000 in the Battle of Fredericksburg. The South lost 5,000.

Burnside was replaced by General Joseph Hooker, who also marched toward Richmond. In May 1863, his army was defeated at the Battle of Chancellorsville by a southern force half its size. The South, however, lost General Stonewall Jackson in the battle.

In the West, Union generals were not so cautious. General Ulysses S. Grant, the most successful of these generals, was a man who took chances. In February 1862, Grant captured Fort Henry, just south of the Kentucky-Tennessee border. Then he took Fort Donelson. These victories opened the South up to invasion from two different water routes. Grant's forces continued south along the Tennessee River to Corinth, Mississippi, an important railroad center.

Before Grant could advance on Corinth, Confederate General Albert Sidney Johnston attacked. On April 6, 1862, he surprised Grant's forces at the town of Shiloh. The Battle of Shiloh was costly for both sides. The South suffered nearly 11,000 casualties. The toll for the North was more than 13,000. However, the Union army was successful in forcing the Confederate army to withdraw from the railroad center, and in the process, it won control of Corinth. The Union now controlled western Tennessee and part of the Mississippi River.

Two weeks after the Battle of Shiloh, Union Commander David Farragut entered the Mississippi River from the Gulf of Mexico and captured New Orleans. By the summer of 1862, the Union controlled almost all of the Mississippi River.

Lesson Summary
EMANCIPATION AND LIFE IN WARTIME

MODIFIED CORNELL NOTES

Northern abolitionists assumed that Lincoln's main war goal was to end slavery because that was what they wanted most. But Lincoln's main goal was to preserve the Union. If that could be done without outlawing slavery, Lincoln would not outlaw slavery. He did not want to free the slaves at the outset of the war because it might provoke the border states into secession. Furthermore, he knew that most northerners did not care enough about slavery to fight a war to end it. Lincoln had no plan to **emancipate**, or free, enslaved people in 1861.

But by mid-1862, Lincoln realized that slavery was important to the southern war effort. Slaves kept farms and factories producing when their owners were away fighting the war. Lincoln decided slavery had to end. On January 1, 1863, Lincoln issued the Emancipation Proclamation.

The proclamation was not the sweeping rejection of slavery abolitionists wanted and expected. It freed slaves only in areas that were fighting the Union. Slaves in border states and the West were not affected, and southern states already under Union control were not affected. States that had seceded did not have to obey the law because they did not recognize the U.S. government. In short, very few slaves were actually freed in 1863.

African Americans in the North were not allowed to fight in the Union army at first. Even after Congress allowed it in 1862, few state governments mobilized African American volunteers. After the Emancipation Proclamation, it was easier for African Americans to enlist. By the end of the war, about 200,000 had served in the army or navy. Over half of these soldiers were former slaves who had escaped or been freed by Union soldiers when they took over southern territory.

Conditions on both sides were horrifying. In most battles, one fourth or more of the soldiers were killed or wounded. Diseases such as pneumonia and malaria killed even more than guns or cannons.

Desertion was a problem for both sides. Between 300,000 and 550,000 Union and Confederate soldiers left their units and went home. Some returned after their crops were planted or harvested. To meet the need for troops, both the North and the South established a **draft**, a system of required military service. The southern draft began in 1862, and the northern draft began in 1863; all eligible men were required to enlist in the army or navy.

(Continues on the next page.)

Lesson Vocabulary

emancipate to set free

draft a law that requires people of a certain age to perform military service

TOPIC 8 LESSON 5

Lesson Summary
EMANCIPATION AND LIFE IN WARTIME

MODIFIED CORNELL NOTES

(Continued from page 107)

People on both sides objected that poor people were fighting the war. Draft riots broke out in many northern cities in 1863 as poor people who could not pay their way out of the draft destroyed draft offices and other property.

While northern industries thrived on war production, the amount of money coming in to the government did not cover the costs of the war. So Congress introduced the first **income tax** in August 1861. This is a tax on the money people receive. Congress also printed $400 million in paper money. This was the first federal paper money, and it led to **inflation**, or a general rise in prices. In the North, prices went up 80 percent on average.

Women in the North and South contributed to the war effort in many ways. Some disguised themselves as men and enlisted in the army, and some were spies. But most women took up the roles their male family members had played in society. Women ran businesses and farms, worked in factories, taught school, and served on the battlefield, in army camps, and in hospitals. Elizabeth Blackwell, the first American woman to earn a medical degree, trained nurses for the Union army. Clara Barton cared for Union soldiers on the battlefield and later founded the American Red Cross.

Lesson Vocabulary

income tax a tax on people's earnings

inflation a rise in prices and a decrease in the value of money

TOPIC 8 LESSON 6

Lesson Summary

THE WAR'S END

Lee determined once more to launch an attack in the North. His forces were outside the town of Gettysburg, Pennsylvania, on July 1, 1863, when they encountered Union troops, now led by General George Meade. Fighting broke out that lasted for three days. When the Battle of Gettysburg was over, the Union had won. The South had lost 28,000 men, and the North had lost 23,000.

The day after the Battle of Gettysburg ended, the city of Vicksburg, Mississippi—one of the last cities on the river still in southern hands—fell to Union General Grant. Grant had laid **siege** to the city for two months. A siege is an attempt to capture a place by surrounding it with troops and cutting it off until its people surrender. Grant's victory at Vicksburg and Lee's defeat at Gettysburg were the turning points of the war, giving the Union an advantage.

On November 19, 1863, President Lincoln attended a ceremony to dedicate a cemetery to those who died at Gettysburg. This became known as the Gettysburg Address. In it, he stressed that "all men are created equal" and that the nation would undergo a "new birth of freedom."

President Lincoln decided to put General Grant in charge of the Union army. Grant marched toward Richmond, fighting a series of battles in Virginia in the spring of 1864 in which he lost many men. Grant knew his men could be replaced, and he also knew that the South was running out of soldiers and supplies.

Another Union general, William Tecumseh Sherman, was driving his army across the South. In his march, he practiced **total war**, or all-out attacks aimed at destroying not only an enemy's army, but also its resources and its people's will to fight. His troops set fire to buildings, seized crops and livestock, and pulled up railroad tracks. Sherman captured Atlanta on September 2, 1864. He then marched east toward the Atlantic Ocean. Sherman's "March to the Sea" brought devastation to a path 60 miles wide.

When Lincoln ran for reelection in 1864, he thought it was likely he would lose. Union chances for a victory remained distant, and many northerners were unhappy with the war. His opponent wanted to compromise with the Confederacy. However, several victories in late 1864 helped Lincoln to win the election.

(Continues on the next page.)

Lesson Vocabulary

siege a military blockade or bombardment of an enemy town or position in order to force it to surrender

total war an all-out war that affects civilians at home as well as soldiers in combat

TOPIC 8 LESSON 6

Lesson Summary
THE WAR'S END

(Continued from page 109)

By March 1865, Grant had extended his armies, encircling Lee. Lee knew that the war was lost. Lincoln knew it too and asked the American people to welcome the South back to the Union. He said, "With malice toward none, [and] charity for all; . . . let us strive together . . . to bind up the nation's wounds."

On April 2, Grant broke the Confederate line and captured Richmond. After briefly retreating west, Lee offered to surrender. On April 9, Grant and Lee met in a home in the town of Appomattox Court House, Virginia, to sign the surrender agreement. The Union generously allowed the Confederates to return home without punishment.

The war was over, but its effects lasted long afterward. Around 250,000 southerners had died, along with over 360,000 northerners.

TOPIC 8 Review Questions
SECTIONALISM AND CIVIL WAR

Answer the questions below using the information in the Lesson Summaries on the previous pages.

Lesson 1: Conflicts and Compromises

1. Explain What was the Wilmot Proviso?

_____

_____

2. What did each side get in the Compromise of 1850?

_____

_____

Lesson 2: Growing Tensions

3. Identify Cause and Effect What were the effects of the Supreme Court's decision in *Dred Scott* v. *Sandford* on Congress, existing law, and slavery?

_____

_____

4. What was the Republican Party's main platform?

_____

_____

Lesson 3: Division and the Outbreak of War

5. Contrast What were the opinions of people in the North and the South about Lincoln's election?

_____

_____

6. Determine Relevance Why was the Confederate capture of Fort Sumter important?

_____

_____

TOPIC 8

Review Questions (continued)

SECTIONALISM AND CIVIL WAR

Lesson 4: The Course of War

7. What were the Union and Confederate war strategies?

_____

_____

8. What was the result of the First Battle of Bull Run?

_____

_____

Lesson 5: Emancipation and Life in Wartime

9. How did Lincoln's war goals change in the early years of the war?

_____

_____

10. **Compare** What problems did the war create for both sides?

_____

_____

Lesson 6: The War's End

11. **Sequence Events** List in chronological order the locations of four Union victories that led to the end of the Civil War.

_____

_____

12. What happened to Confederate soldiers under the terms of the surrender agreement?

_____

_____

TOPIC 9
Note Taking Study Guide
THE RECONSTRUCTION ERA

Focus Question: After the Civil War, what were the goals of the newly-freed slaves in the South? What barriers did they face to achieving these goals?

As you read, note specific political and social goals in the years following the Civil War. Describe actions taken to accomplish these goals. Indicate what resulted from these actions.

Goal	Action	Outcome
Prevent the South from rebelling again.		
	Freedmen's Bureaus were established.	
		Over objections of President Johnson, the Fourteenth Amendment passed, giving citizenship to all persons born in the United States.
Guarantee political and social equality for African Americans.		

TOPIC 9 LESSON 1

Lesson Summary
EARLY RECONSTRUCTION

MODIFIED CORNELL NOTES

As the Civil War ended, enormous problems faced the nation. Much of the South lay in ruins, the homeless needed food and shelter, and many in the North and South harbored hard feelings toward their former foes. The process of bringing the North and the South back together again, known as Reconstruction, would occupy the nation for years to come.

Lincoln and some fellow Republicans thought a **lenient** Reconstruction policy would strengthen the Republican Party in the South. The Radical Republicans disagreed and claimed only a "hard," or strict, Reconstruction policy would keep the South from rising again.

It was urgent to deal with the needs of the **freedmen**, or enslaved people who had been freed by war, as well as other war refugees. Congress created the Freedmen's Bureau in March of 1865. The bureau's first duty was to provide emergency relief to people displaced by war.

The Freedmen's Bureau set up schools to teach freedmen to read and write, and it helped to start schools at which African Americans could extend their education. The Freedmen's Bureau also helped freedmen find jobs and settled disputes between blacks and whites.

As the war drew to a close, President Lincoln hoped for a peaceful Reconstruction. But Lincoln had no chance to put his plans into practice. He was shot on April 14, 1865, by John Wilkes Booth, a Confederate sympathizer. Lincoln died a few hours later.

News of Lincoln's death shocked the nation. His successor as President was Andrew Johnson, who was from Tennessee. A southern Democrat who had remained loyal to the Union, Johnson had expressed bitterness toward the Confederates. Many expected him to take a hard line on Reconstruction.

Like President Lincoln, Andrew Johnson wanted to restore the Union quickly and easily, so he proposed a lenient plan for Reconstruction. Johnson's plan required southern states to ratify the Thirteenth Amendment, which banned slavery and forced labor. His plan also offered amnesty to most Confederates and allowed southern states to form new governments and to elect representatives to Congress.

Lesson Vocabulary

lenient gentle; not harsh or strict

freedmen the men and women who had been enslaved

TOPIC 9 LESSON 2 — Lesson Summary
RADICAL RECONSTRUCTION

Congress rejected Johnson's plan and appointed a committee to form a new plan for the South. The committee learned that some southern states had passed **black codes**, or laws to control African Americans. In response, Congress adopted a harder line against the South. The Radical Republicans took the hardest stance. They wanted to prevent former Confederates from regaining control of southern politics, and they wanted to make sure that freedmen had the right to vote.

The struggle for Reconstruction was focused on the President and Congress during 1866. Congress passed the Civil Rights Act of 1866, but President Johnson vetoed it and another bill extending the Freedmen's Bureau. Congress overturned both vetoes.

Congress also drew up the Fourteenth Amendment, which declared all people born or naturalized in the United States to be citizens. It barred the states from passing laws to take away a citizen's rights. The Fourteenth Amendment also stopped states from taking away property or liberty "without due process of law." In addition, any state that stopped its adult males from voting would have its representation in Congress reduced. Despite opposition from President Johnson, the amendment was ratified in 1868.

As the elections of 1866 approached, violence directed at African Americans erupted in southern cities. Outrage at this violence led Congress to push a stricter form of Reconstruction, called Radical Reconstruction. The Reconstruction Act of 1867 threw out the governments of all states that refused to adopt the Fourteenth Amendment. It also imposed military rule on these states. By June of 1868, all of these states had ratified the Fourteenth Amendment and written new constitutions. They also allowed African Americans to vote.

Meanwhile, the Radical Republicans **impeached** and tried to convict President Johnson in order to remove him from office. To impeach means to bring formal charges against an elected official. Johnson barely escaped removal by one vote.

Ulysses S. Grant won the presidential election for the Republicans in 1868. With the South under military rule, some 500,000 African Americans voted. Grant was a war hero and a moderate with support from many northern business owners. Radicals then began to lose their grip on the Republican Party.

Despite Democratic opposition, Congress approved the Fifteenth Amendment in 1869. It barred all states from denying the right to vote "on account of race, color, or previous condition of servitude."

Lesson Vocabulary

black codes the southern laws that severely limited the rights of African Americans after the Civil War

impeach to bring charges of serious wrongdoing against a public official

Lesson Summary
RECONSTRUCTION AND SOUTHERN SOCIETY

MODIFIED CORNELL NOTES

For the first time, African Americans in the South played an important role in politics, serving as sheriffs, mayors, judges, and legislators. Sixteen African Americans served in the House of Representatives and two served in the Senate. Some other accomplishments of Radical Reconstruction included public schools opening in southern states, evenly spread taxation, and property rights for women. Bridges, roads, and buildings destroyed by the war were rebuilt.

Angry at being shut out of power, some whites resorted to violence. They formed secret societies, such as the Ku Klux Klan, to terrorize African Americans and their white allies. Congress passed laws **barring** the use of force against voters, but the damage had been done. In the face of threats and violence from the Klan and other groups, voting by African Americans declined. The stage was set for the end of Reconstruction.

Support for Radical Republicans declined as Americans shifted focus from the Civil War to their own lives. Many northerners lost faith in the Republicans and their policies as Grant's presidency suffered from controversy and corruption.

With the end of Reconstruction, African Americans began losing their remaining political and civil rights in the South. Southern whites passed a number of laws to prevent blacks from voting. Because these laws could apply to blacks and whites, they did not violate the Fifteenth Amendment.

At the time of emancipation, most freedmen were very poor. Many in rural areas became sharecroppers. A **sharecropper** is a farmer who rents land and pays a share of each year's crop as rent. Sharecroppers hoped to save money and eventually buy land of their own. But weather conditions and the ups and downs of crop prices often caused sharecroppers to lose money and become locked in a cycle of debt. They would then become poorer and poorer each year.

Lesson Vocabulary

bar prevent or prohibit

sharecropper a person who rents a plot of land from another person and farms it in exchange for a share of the crop

Lesson Summary
THE AFTERMATH OF RECONSTRUCTION

The end of Reconstruction was finalized with the election of Rutherford B. Hayes in 1876. Although he was a Republican, he vowed to end Reconstruction to avoid a challenge to his election by Democrats. Hayes removed all federal troops from the South.

Southerners passed laws that were designed to limit African American political participation. A **poll tax**, or a tax to be paid before voting, kept many blacks and poor whites from voting. Another law required voters to pass a **literacy test**, or a test to see if a person could read or write, before voting. Most southern blacks had not been educated and could not pass the test. In addition, whites whose fathers or grandfathers could vote in the South on January 1, 1867, did not have to take the test.

Southern states created laws, known as Jim Crow laws, requiring **segregation**, or enforced separation of races. In *Plessy* v. *Ferguson*, the Supreme Court ruled that laws could require "separate" facilities as long as they were "equal." The "separate but equal" rule was in effect until the 1950s, but the facilities for African Americans were rarely equal.

During Reconstruction, the South's economy slowly began to recover. By the 1880s, new industries appeared. Agriculture was the first industry to recover, with cotton production setting new records by 1875. Farmers also started to put more land into tobacco production, and output grew.

Industries that turn raw materials into finished products, such as the textile industry, came to play an important role in the South's economy. New mills and factories also grew to use the South's natural resources, such as iron, timber, and oil. By 1900, the South was no longer dependent on "King Cotton." A "New South" based on manufacturing was emerging.

Lesson Vocabulary

poll tax a tax required before a person can vote

literacy test an examination to see if a person can read and write; used in the past to restrict voting rights

segregation the legal separation of people based on racial, ethnic, or other differences

Name_____ Class_____ Date_____

Answer the questions below using the information in the Lesson Summaries on the previous pages.

Lesson 1: Early Reconstruction

1. **Identify Central Issues** Name two problems that faced the nation during Reconstruction.

_____

_____

2. How did the Freedmen's Bureau help former slaves?

_____

_____

Lesson 2: Radical Reconstruction

3. What were two goals of the Radical Republicans?

_____

_____

4. **Identify Cause and Effect** What did some southern states do as a result of the Reconstruction Act of 1867?

_____

_____

Lesson 3: Reconstruction and Southern Society

5. Name three accomplishments of Reconstruction in the South.

_____

_____

6. **Describe** How did the rights of African Americans in the South change after the end of Radical Reconstruction?

_____

_____

Lesson 4: The Aftermath of Reconstruction

7. **Cite Evidence** Describe the laws passed by southern states that demonstrate their intent to limit the rights of African Americans.

_____

_____

8. What development led to the emergence of a "New South"?

_____

_____

Name_____ Class_____ Date_____

Focus Question: What factors led to changes in the American West in the late 1800s, and what were the results of those changes?

As you read, focus upon the settlement and economic development of the American West in the late 1800s. Identify several developments and actions that contributed to the shift of people to the West and the way settlers and business leaders chose to use the region's resources. Then record some consequences of that settlement and economic development for the West and other regions of the United States. A few bullet points have been provided, but you will need to add more.

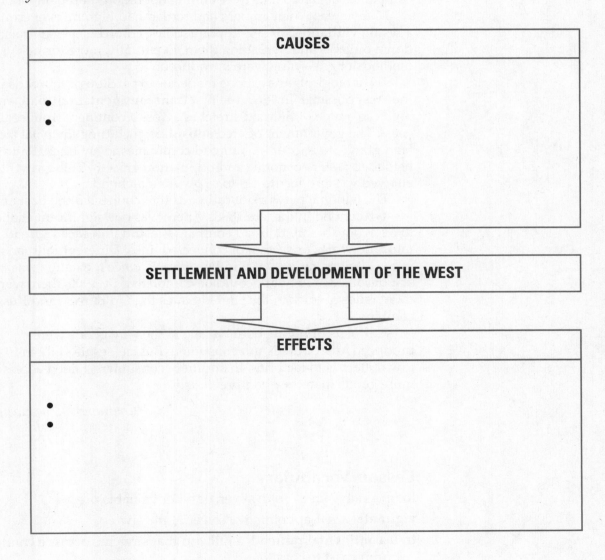

CAUSES

-
-

SETTLEMENT AND DEVELOPMENT OF THE WEST

EFFECTS

-
-

Name_____ Class_____ Date_____

MODIFIED CORNELL NOTES

The California gold rush began a western mining boom in the mid-1800s. Miners hoped to strike a **lode**, or rich vein of gold or silver. One such lode was discovered by Henry Comstock in Nevada in 1859. This and other finds in Colorado, South Dakota, and Alaska helped fuel massive population growth. Many boomtowns sprang up across the West.

Very few miners ever got rich. Most of the gold and silver required large machinery to get it out of the ground. Large companies began to take over mining operations and paid laborers.

Many areas where miners had settled had high rates of crime. As a result, **vigilantes**, or self-appointed law enforcers, began tracking down outlaws and punishing them. Eventually, more formal methods of governing were introduced.

Technological innovations made the expansion of railroads into the West possible. In 1863, the first **transcontinental railroad** was built. This type of railroad stretches across a continent from coast to coast. The government offered **subsidies**, including financial aid or land grants, to encourage railroad companies to lay track. Railroads helped to foster economic and population growth. This growth allowed western territories to apply for statehood.

The national network of railroads that connected the East and the West expanded in the late 1800s. There was one significant challenge to overcome before railroad companies could link each railroad into a **network**, or system of connected lines. Different railroads used different gauges, or widths, of track. Once the gauge was standardized, a network could be completed. By 1900, there were more miles of track in the United States than in Europe and Russia combined.

Railroads brought about change in the way goods were produced, distributed, and consumed. Businesses used them to ship raw materials to factories. In addition, consumers gained access to more goods than they had previously.

(Continues on the next page.)

Lesson Vocabulary

lode a rich vein of gold, silver, or other valuable ore

vigilante a self-appointed enforcer of the law

transcontinental railroad a railroad that stretches across a continent from coast to coast

subsidy a land grant or other financial help from the government

network a system of connected railroad lines

(Continued from page 120)

Competition between railroads was fierce. Rate wars broke out, causing companies to lose money. Many were forced to offer **rebates**, or discounts, to their biggest customers. Railroads looked for ways to end competition. One method was to form a **pool**. In a pool, several companies agree to divide up a business area. This allows them to fix prices at a higher level. Farmers reacted to high railroad rates by pushing for government regulations.

The development of railroads made the expansion of industry after 1865 possible. Building them created thousands of jobs for steelworkers, lumberjacks, and miners. They also opened much more of the country to settlement and growth.

Lesson Vocabulary

rebate a discount

pool a system in which several railroad companies agreed to divide up the business in an area and set prices

Lesson Summary
WESTERN AGRICULTURE

MODIFIED CORNELL NOTES

In the 1860s, cattle ranching grew rapidly on the Great Plains. Wild cattle, known as longhorns, roamed freely across Texas. Longhorns could travel far on little water and could live off of the grass that grew on the plains. Texas ranchers drove the animals north on **cattle drives** to railroad lines in Kansas and Missouri. Cowhands led these drives. They worked nearly 18-hour days and were paid low wages.

Cattle drives ended in **cow towns**. These were towns that had sprung up along railroad lines. Cattle were held in large pens until they could be loaded and shipped to markets in the East. As the towns grew, stores opened to provide goods and services to the population.

In the 1870s, ranching spread north from Texas all the way to Montana. Investors **poured** millions of dollars into the West, which helped fuel a cattle boom. This boom was temporary, however. Farmers began moving onto the range and fencing in their fields. After a time, there was not enough grass on the open range to feed all the cattle. Ranchers were forced to buy land and fence it in.

By 1900, approximately 500,000 Americans had set up farms under the Homestead Act. This act promised 160 acres of free land to qualified individuals who agreed to stay on the land for five years. Large land-owning companies took much of the land illegally, however, and resold it to farmers at a higher price.

The Morrill Land-Grant Colleges Act of 1862 offered states a federal land grant to build schools teaching farming and engineering. States received 30,000 acres of public land per congressional representative. Then, in 1890, a second Morrill Act was passed. This required states to admit African American students or to build separate land-grant colleges for them.

Life on the plains was hard. Many settlers lived in **sod houses**, which were made of soil held together by grass roots. Rain often leaked through the roofs. Dry weather increased the risk of fire during the summer, and the lack of trees and hills caused huge snowdrifts to build up during winter. Homesteaders depended on the environment for their livelihood. This meant they had to become nearly self-sufficient.

(Continues on the next page.)

Lesson Vocabulary

cattle drives the herding and moving of cattle, usually to railroad lines

cow towns a settlement that grew up at the end of a cattle trail

pour to move or proceed in great quantity

sod houses a house built of soil held together by grass roots

TOPIC 10 LESSON 2

Lesson Summary
WESTERN AGRICULTURE

(Continued from page 122)

During the 1860s, farmers began to cooperate. In 1867, they formed the National Grange to help boost profits and reduce railroad rates. The Farmers' Alliance formed in the 1870s. Similar to the Grange, its members set up **cooperatives**. These were groups of farmers who pooled their money together to buy seeds and tools in large quantities.

In 1892, farmers and labor unions joined together to form the People's Party, also known as the Populist Party. They wanted the government to regulate railroad rates, create an income tax, and limit the workday to eight hours. They also called for "free silver," which would require silver mined in the West to be coined into money. This was because they believed that low farm prices were a result of not having enough money in circulation.

Lesson Vocabulary

cooperative a group of people who pool their money to buy or sell goods wholesale

TOPIC 10 LESSON 3	**Lesson Summary**
	HARDSHIP FOR NATIVE AMERICANS

MODIFIED CORNELL NOTES

The American Indians living on the Great Plains had rich and varied cultures. Many had well-organized religions and warrior societies. The horse was introduced by the Spanish in the 1400s. After the Pueblo Indians **revolted** against the Spanish in the 1600s, they obtained horses that they traded with the Plains tribes. Plains Indians used the horse to hunt and also to move.

Horses allowed Plains cultures to follow buffalo herds. They began living in **tepees**, or tents made from buffalo skins stretched across tall poles. The buffalo became the center of Plains Indian culture. They used it for food, clothing, and shelter.

Men had the responsibility of waging war to protect their people or to defend or extend their territory. They also hunted and served as religious leaders. Women oversaw life in the home. They gathered food, cared for children, and engaged in crafts.

Plains Indians had fought among themselves before the arrival of Europeans and Americans. However, as settlers began taking their lands, conflicts broke out with settlers. The United States government made several peace agreements with different tribes, but often broke them. Then, it signed treaties with Plains Indians that required them to live on specific areas of land, known as **reservations**.

After being defeated by the United States Army in 1868, the Lakota signed such a treaty. When gold was discovered in the Black Hills region of the Lakota reservation, however, thousands of miners rushed to the area. Conflict broke out between Indian warriors and Colonel George A. Custer at the Battle of Little Bighorn in 1876. The Lakota defeated Custer at Little Big Horn, but they were eventually forced to give up about one third of their reservation land. Other Indian groups in the Northwest and Southwest also fought against the United States government. They were eventually defeated.

(Continues on the next page.)

Lesson Vocabulary

revolt to rise up against authority and fight

tepees a tent made by stretching buffalo skins on tall poles

reservation a limited area of land set aside for Native Americans

TOPIC 10 LESSON 3

Lesson Summary
HARDSHIP FOR NATIVE AMERICANS

(Continued from page 124)

For many American Indians, the loss of their lands to settlers meant that they lost their way of life. Some practiced the Ghost Dance, which celebrated a time when Indians would live freely again on the Plains. Settlers mistook dance ceremonies as war preparations, which led to the massacre at Wounded Knee, another tragic confrontation between Lakotas and the United States Army in which hundreds of Lakotas died.

Some whites and many American Indians began to speak out against the loss of their way of life. Still, the United States government wanted Indians to adopt white ways and become farmers. Congress passed the Dawes Act in 1887, which divided up some reservations to provide farmland to individual families. Much of the land was unsuitable for farming. Many Indians ended up selling their land to whites at low prices.

Name_____ Class_____ Date_____

MODIFIED CORNELL NOTES

Just prior to the Civil War, a new method for making steel was discovered, which came to be known as the Bessemer process. This process made it cheaper to make steel, which was stronger and less likely to rust than iron. After the Civil War, railroad companies began to lay new track using steel rails. This spurred the rapid growth of the steel industry and supported the growth of **industrial** towns such as Pittsburgh throughout the Midwest.

A Scottish immigrant, Andrew Carnegie, opened a steel mill and used the profits to buy out rivals and other important industries related to steel production. He soon gained control of all phases of steel production from mining to shipping finished steel, a practice known as **vertical integration**. This enabled Carnegie to amass a sizable fortune and dominate the U.S. steel industry.

The railroad boom made it possible for large factories, which produced goods more cheaply than small ones, to bring their goods to markets across the nation. In order to continue growing, these companies had to increase their capital. Some invested their own revenue, while others borrowed from investors or sold them **stock**, or shares of the company. Many businesses formed as **corporations**, which are owned by investors. Stockholders often received **dividends**, or shares of a corporation's profit. As American industry continued to grow, bankers who loaned corporations money made large profits. One such banker was J.P. Morgan, who in the early 1900s used his profits to buy up troubled corporations and merge them into a single large corporation, the United States Steel Company. This process reduced competition and ensured large profits.

(Continues on the next page.)

Lesson Vocabulary

industrial having factories that make products

vertical integration practice in which a single manufacturer controls all of the steps used to change raw materials into finished products

stock share of ownership in a corporation

corporations business that is owned by investors whose risk of loss is limited

dividends share of a corporation's profit

(Continued from page 126)

John D. Rockefeller, who founded Standard Oil in 1870, used similar tactics to build his oil empire. He reduced competition by buying up other oil refineries and combining them into the Standard Oil Company of Ohio. He then reduced his prices and forced railroad companies to grant rebates to his company, giving him a distinct advantage over other producers. In an effort to increase his control over the industry, he formed the Standard Oil Trust in 1882, which was a group of corporations run by a single board of directors. Trusts worked by forcing smaller companies to turn over their stock in exchange for stock in the newly created trust, which paid them dividends. The result was that Rockefeller formed a **monopoly**, which is a single entity that controls all or most of the business of an industry.

Some Americans criticized monopolies and trusts because they believed such practices were abuses of the **free enterprise system**, which relies on competition. Because monopolies reduced competition, critics believed monopolies and trusts had no need to keep prices low or work to improve their products. They also believed the wealth amassed by these entities would be used to influence political leaders' decisions. As a result, Congress passed the Sherman Antitrust Act in 1890, banning the formation of trusts and monopolies. In their defense, large corporations argued that they were able to produce goods more cheaply, leading to lower prices for consumers and higher wages for workers.

Lesson Vocabulary

monopoly a company or group having control of all or nearly all of the business of an industry

free enterprise system economic system in which businesses are owned by private citizens who decide what to produce, how much to produce, and what prices to charge

TOPIC 10 LESSON 5

Lesson Summary
THE LABOR MOVEMENT

MODIFIED CORNELL NOTES

The rise of industry brought significant changes for workers. High rates of immigration and the increasing use of machinery made it easier for factory owners to replace workers. Easily replaced workers found it hard to bargain for higher wages, and many people—especially women and children—were forced to work in sweatshops, or cramped, unsafe workplaces. Laborers worked long hours for low wages and faced the constant threat of illness, injury, or death.

Some workers fought back by slowing their work pace or holding strikes, but most early efforts to form unions failed. In 1869, a union known as the Knights of Labor formed for skilled workers. Within a decade, it had opened its membership to immigrants, African Americans, women, and unskilled workers. The union held public rallies and meetings to call for shortening the workday, ending child labor, guaranteeing equal pay for men and women, and forcing employers to share ownership and profits with workers. Membership levels increased dramatically after a strike in 1885 forced a railroad company to raise wages that it had previously cut, even though the Knights of Labor did not support the strike.

However, membership levels dropped sharply the following year, after multiple episodes of violence occurred when workers at the McCormick Harvester Company in Chicago went on strike. After the McCormick Company hired strikebreakers to replace striking workers, conflict erupted outside the factory, and police ended up killing four workers. The next day, a group of anarchists gathered in Haymarket Square to protest the killings. A bomb exploded, killing seven police officers. This caused many Americans to believe unions were controlled by anarchists, and membership levels dropped.

(Continues on the next page.)

Lesson Vocabulary

sweatshop workplace where people labor long hours in poor conditions for low pay

strikebreaker replacement for a striking worker

anarchist person who opposes organized government

Name_____ Class_____ Date_____

MODIFIED CORNELL NOTES

(Continued from page 128)

A new union formed in 1886, known as the American Federation of Labor (AFL). This was an organization comprised of many different **trade unions**, which were unions of persons working in the same trade or line of work. The AFL supported the use of strikes and **collective bargaining**, or the right of unions to negotiate with employers on behalf of workers. Even though African Americans, immigrants, and unskilled workers were not allowed to join, membership grew by ten times within 25 years.

The International Ladies' Garment Workers Union (ILGWU) formed in 1900 and became part of the AFL. In 1909, it launched a successful strike, forcing employers to raise wages and shorten the workday. However, most women did not belong to unions and continued to work long hours in unsafe conditions. Some states began to pass laws to protect factory workers after a fire broke out in the Triangle Shirtwaist Factory—a sweatshop in New York City—in 1911. Approximately 150 people—mostly women—died because they could not get out. The company had put chains on the doors to keep workers at their jobs.

Lesson Vocabulary

trade union an association of trade workers formed to gain higher wages and better working conditions

collective bargaining process by which a union representing a group of workers negotiates with management for a contract

TOPIC 10 LESSON 6

Lesson Summary
NEW TECHNOLOGIES

From 1860 to 1900, over 500,000 new **patents** guaranteeing inventors the right to profit from their inventions were issued by the United States Patent Office. Many of these patents were for new inventions that helped industries grow and made daily life easier for many Americans. One of these inventions—the typewriter—changed the way business was conducted. It allowed people to create documents quickly that could be read more easily than handwritten documents.

Governments and members of society also benefited from faster communication. During the 1850s, Cyrus Field led efforts to lay a **transatlantic** cable for sending telegraphs between Europe and the United States. After several unsuccessful attempts, the first telegraph was sent by Queen Victoria to President James Buchanan in 1858. Although the cable broke, a stronger cable was laid between the continents in 1866.

Another improvement in communications came with Alexander Graham Bell's invention of the telephone in 1876. Unlike the earlier telegraph — which sent electrical signals that were interpreted as dots and dashes and later decoded into messages — the telephone could transmit voices over wires. Although many people initially considered it a toy, by 1885 Bell had sold more than 300,000 telephones, mostly to businesses. Because businesses did not have to go to the telegraph office, they could get information or place orders even faster.

Thomas Edison's laboratory at Menlo Park, New Jersey, introduced several new inventions that changed everyday life for most Americans, including the light bulb, phonograph, and motion picture projector. He later built the first power plant in New York City's business district, bringing electricity with the flip of a switch. Businesses began relying on electricity for power and light, while factories replaced steam-powered engines with electric engines. Electric-powered streetcars transported people through city streets. As a result, the modern age of electricity began.

Meanwhile, Gustavus Swift's invention of refrigeration in the 1880s changed the American food industry. He built a meatpacking plant in Chicago, which allowed animals transported by rail to be sent to the plant, butchered, and then packed in refrigerated railroad cars to be brought to markets around the nation.

(Continues on the next page.)

Lesson Vocabulary
patent license for a new invention
transatlantic crossing or spanning the Atlantic Ocean

MODIFIED CORNELL NOTES

(Continued from page 130)

Several inventions turned pastimes that only the wealthy could afford into everyday activities for Americans. One such invention was George Eastman's lightweight Kodak camera. This camera was much less bulky than previous photographic equipment and photography quickly developed into a popular pastime. Similarly, Henry Ford's invention of the **moving assembly line** allowed workers to dramatically reduce the amount of time needed to produce automobiles. This increase in efficiency allowed Ford to **mass-produce** cars, making them more affordable for the average consumer. Although many people avoided cars at first—believing them to be dangerous—by 1917, there were over 4.5 million cars on American roads.

Another invention that revolutionized transportation was the airplane. Orville and Wilbur Wright had successfully tested their invention in 1903, and within several years had built a plane that could stay in the air for up to half an hour. Many Americans did not see the plane as a practical invention, but the U.S. military took interest when they realized planes could be used to locate enemy positions on battlefields. Eventually, the plane changed everyday life by shortening the time required for travel and trade.

Lesson Vocabulary

moving assembly line method of production in which workers stay in one place as products pass along a track or moving belt

mass-produce make large quantities of a product quickly and cheaply

TOPIC 10 — Review Questions
INDUSTRIAL AND ECONOMIC GROWTH

Answer the questions below using the information in the Lesson Summaries on the previous pages.

Lesson 1: Mining, Railroads, and the Economy

1. What did the government do to encourage the building of the first transcontinental railroad?

_____

_____

2. **Cause and Effect** How did the building of a national railroad network change America?

_____

_____

Lesson 2: Western Agriculture

3. Why was the era of the great cattle drives so short-lived?

_____

_____

4. **Identify Details** Name two things that the Populist Party wanted.

_____

_____

Lesson 3: Hardship for Native Americans

5. How did the Plains Indians' way of life change once they obtained horses?

_____

_____

6. **Identify Main Ideas and Details** What was the goal of the Dawes Act, and how did it affect the Plains Indians?

_____

_____

_____

TOPIC 10 **Review Questions** (continued)

INDUSTRIAL AND ECONOMIC GROWTH

Lesson 4: Industry and Corporations

7. Why did some American businesses in the late 1800s decide to become corporations?

_____

_____

8. Compare and Contrast Describe the different positions that critics and defenders had about big business.

_____

_____

Lesson 5: The Labor Movement

9. What were the goals of the Knights of Labor?

_____

_____

10. Compare and Contrast What were some major differences between the Knights of Labor and the American Federation of Labor?

_____

_____

Lesson 6: New Technologies

11. How did Henry Ford make the automobile affordable to millions of people?

_____

_____

12. Categorize Which inventions improved communications? Which improved transportation?

_____

_____

TOPIC 11	Note Taking Study Guide
	THE PROGRESSIVE ERA

Focus Question: What social, political, and economic changes transformed American society in the late 1800s and early 1900s, and what reforms did reformers promote to address those changes?

As you read, focus upon the way the population and ways of life in the United States changed in the late 1800s and early 1900s. Identify those changes. Then identify the solutions that Progressives and other reformers achieved and proposed to address the problems that they saw arising from those changes. A few bullet points have been provided, but you will need to add more.

Changes to American Society	Reforms
•	•
•	•
•	•
•	

TOPIC 11 LESSON 1

Lesson Summary
A NEW WAVE OF IMMIGRATION

From 1865 to 1915, over 25 million immigrants traveled to what they saw as a "land of opportunity," a land full of economic opportunity where individuals had rights protected by law. Many were driven from their homelands by **push factors** such as scarcity of land or religious **persecution**. Others were attracted to the United States by **pull factors** such as available factory jobs.

Making the journey was challenging. Many immigrants could only afford to stay in **steerage**, a level of crowded airless rooms below deck, as the immigrant ships made their journey across the ocean. Disease often spread rapidly.

For most European immigrants, the long journey ended at Ellis Island near New York. They had to pass a medical inspection in order to enter the country. After 1910, most Asian immigrants were processed on Angel Island in San Francisco Bay. Some immigrants experienced long delays in processing or were deported back to their country of origin.

Immigrants during the 1800s and early 1900s came in two primary waves. The "old immigrants" had mostly come from northern and western European countries such as England, Ireland, or Germany. This pattern changed during the late 1800s. After 1885, a wave of "new immigrants" came from southern and eastern European countries such as Italy, Poland, and Russia. Others came from Asian countries such as China and Japan.

Many immigrants stayed in the cities where they landed, settling in neighborhoods with others from the same ethnic group. Separated from mainstream American culture by language and religion, immigrants had to adapt through **acculturation**. This is the process of adapting to a new culture while holding onto older traditions. For example, many kept their traditional religions, family structures, and community life while learning to use American institutions such as schools and the political system. Some groups blended English with their native language.

(Continues on the next page.)

Lesson Vocabulary

push factor a condition that drives people from their homeland

persecution the mistreatment or punishment of a group of people because of their beliefs

pull factor a condition that attracts people to move to a new area

steerage on a ship, the cramped quarters for passengers paying the lowest fares

acculturation process of holding on to old traditions while adapting to a new culture

TOPIC 11 LESSON 1
Lesson Summary
A NEW WAVE OF IMMIGRATION

(Continued from page 135)

While immigrants tried to acculturate, some Americans known as **nativists** wanted to limit immigration. Nativists feared that immigrants were too different to learn how to fit into American culture and that they would take away job opportunities. As a result of anti-immigrant sentiment, Congress passed several laws limiting immigration. In 1882, it passed the Chinese Exclusion Act, banning Chinese laborers from immigrating to the United States, and in 1917, it passed a law denying entry to any immigrant who was unable to read his or her own language.

Lesson Vocabulary

nativist a person opposed to immigration

Name_____ Class_____ Date_____

MODIFIED CORNELL NOTES

During the 1800s, industrialization fueled the process of **urbanization**, or movement to cities. As industries grew, city factories required more workers, drawing both immigrants and rural farmers. Many African Americans began migrating to northern cities to escape prejudice and violence in the South, forming growing communities in northern cities. By 1890, approximately 33 percent of Americans lived in urban areas.

Cities became increasingly stratified. Most poor families clustered near the city's center. Many lived in **tenements**, small apartments often with no windows, heat, or indoor bathrooms. Often, up to 10 people had to share a single room. Business owners built factories near city centers to take advantage of rail connections and cheap labor. Despite the poor conditions, city slums grew rapidly. Members of the middle class tended to live outside city centers. They lived in their own homes on streets shaded by trees. They joined clubs and pursued **leisure** activities. Outbreaks of disease, while still a threat, were much less frequent than in the slums. The wealthy lived in mansions protected by walls or gates, holding lavish parties and modeling their lives on those of European nobles.

Rapid urbanization led to increasing levels of crime and pollution in cities. In response to pressure from reformers, city governments began to pass **building codes**, which set standards for construction and safety. They hired workers to pick up garbage and created professional fire and police forces. They also passed zoning laws to keep factories out of neighborhoods where people lived. Many cities also built public transportation systems.

Religious groups and organizations such as the Salvation Army and Catholic Church worked to help the poor while Protestant ministers began preaching a new Social Gospel, which called on well-to-do Christians to help the poor. Merchants and industrialists were encouraged to give workers enough pay to support families and grant them additional time off. Other organizations formed to support the needs of women, youth, or specific ethnic groups.

(Continues on the next page.)

Lesson Vocabulary

urbanization the movement of population from farms to cities

tenement a small apartment in a city slum building

leisure fun things you do when you are not working

building code a standard set by the government for building construction and safety

TOPIC 11 LESSON 2

Lesson Summary
URBANIZATION

(Continued from page 137)

To ease the plight of the poor, reformers such as Jane Addams organized **settlement houses**, community centers that offered services to the poor such as education, child care, and recreational activities. These reformers typically lived in the neighborhoods where they worked. By 1900, approximately 100 settlement houses had opened in American cities.

Lesson Vocabulary

settlement house a community center organized, beginning in the late 1800s, to offer services to the poor

TOPIC 11 LESSON 3

Lesson Summary
THE RISE OF PROGRESSIVISM

The Gilded Age, which lasted from the 1870s through the 1890s, was a period marked by political corruption and extravagant spending. Many Americans became increasingly concerned that rich bankers, industrialists, and other wealthy men were using their power to control politics at the expense of the greater good. People were also concerned about corruption.

Politicians known as **political bosses** gained power over many city, county, and state governments. They took payoffs from local businesses and controlled local job markets—often providing jobs to the poor in exchange for votes for the boss or his chosen candidate. Despite their corruption, such bosses were popular with the urban poor, particularly immigrants. For example, when Boss William Tweed—who controlled New York City—died in jail in 1878, thousands of poor New Yorkers mourned him.

One source of corruption was the spoils system. Based on **patronage**—the practice of giving jobs to political supporters—the spoils system had grown since the early 1800s. Many officeholders lacked the skills to do their jobs correctly, and some stole from the government. Reformers stepped up their efforts to end the spoils system after President James Garfield was assassinated in 1881 for rejecting it. By passing the Pendleton Act in 1883, Congress created a Civil Service Commission to make sure that only qualified people got jobs with the federal government. By 1900, it controlled about 40 percent of all federal jobs.

The government also tried to **regulate** big business. It set up the Interstate Commerce Commission, or ICC. The ICC made sure that railroads did not engage in unfair practices, such as reducing competition. In 1890, Congress passed a law to regulate **trusts**, or large corporations that controlled industries. The Sherman Antitrust Act made it illegal for businesses to limit competition. Although government efforts were weak at first, attempts to regulate big business slowly gained strength.

(Continues on the next page.)

Lesson Vocabulary

political boss a powerful politician who controls government, trades favors for support, and demands payoffs from businesses

patronage the practice of awarding government jobs to political supporters

regulate to set rules that control business or other economic activity, usually to protect the public

trust group of corporations run by a single board of directors

Name_____ Class_____ Date_____

MODIFIED CORNELL NOTES

(Continued from page 139)

Reformers who tried to replace corrupt officials with honest leaders were called Progressives. They believed that the problems of society could be solved and wanted the government to act in the **public interest**. The late 1800s and early 1900s are called the Progressive Era. The Progressives were helped by the press. Some reporters began to describe the horrible conditions in poor areas of cities. Others exposed the unfair practices of some big businesses. These journalists became known as **muckrakers**. They helped turn public opinion in favor of reform.

Progressives wanted the government to act for the good of the people. They especially promoted education and democratic values. Many Progressives wanted voters to have more power. A number of states passed measures to achieve this goal. Most states began to hold **primaries**, or elections to choose a party's candidate for a general election. In the past, party leaders had picked candidates. Other changes included the **initiative**, **referendum**, and **recall**. These were political processes that gave voters power to initiate legislation, vote directly on a bill, or remove an elected official from office, respectively.

Lesson Vocabulary

public interest the good of the people

muckraker a journalist who exposed corruption and bad business practices in the late 1800s and early 1900s

primary an election in which voters choose their party's candidate for the general election

initiative a process by which voters can put a bill directly before the state legislature

referendum a process by which people vote directly on a bill

recall a process by which voters can remove an elected official from office

Lesson Summary
THE PROGRESSIVE PRESIDENTS

When President William McKinley was assassinated in 1901, Vice President Theodore Roosevelt took office. Roosevelt thought that trusts could be good or bad. He wanted the government to stop bad trusts. Bad trusts abused workers or cheated the public. In 1902, he had the government bring a lawsuit against Northern Securities. The lawsuit charged that the company was trying to limit trade. Such actions were illegal according to the Sherman Antitrust Act. The Supreme Court agreed with Roosevelt. It ordered the trust to be broken up. The President then took similar actions against other trusts.

President Roosevelt supported a number of other reforms. Unlike earlier Presidents, he sided with labor unions in their disputes with big businesses. When he ran for President in 1904, Roosevelt promised Americans a Square Deal. By this he meant that all Americans should have the same opportunities to succeed. He sent government inspectors into meatpacking houses. He attacked drug companies that made false claims. Roosevelt also believed in conservation, the protection of natural resources. While Roosevelt was President, the government set aside 194,000 acres of land to create national parks.

Roosevelt's successor, William Howard Taft, had the support of Progressives until he agreed to raise tariffs. Progressives also accused him of blocking conservation efforts. In the election of 1912, Roosevelt ran against Taft and Woodrow Wilson. Because Roosevelt and Taft split the Republican vote, Wilson, a Democrat, won.

Wilson's main goal was to increase competition in the economy. He persuaded Congress to create the Federal Trade Commission, or FTC. The FTC had the power to investigate businesses and order them to stop using practices that destroyed their competition. Wilson also supported laws that regulated banks.

Lesson Vocabulary

conservation the protection of natural resources

national park an area set aside by the federal government for people to visit

TOPIC 11 — LESSON 5

Lesson Summary

PROGRESS AND SETBACKS FOR JUSTICE

In the late 1800s and early 1900s, women continued their efforts to win the right to vote. They organized marches, met with elected officials, **picketed**, and even went to jail. **Suffragists**, or people who campaigned for women's right to vote, were active all around the country. Their work resulted in the passage of the Nineteenth Amendment in 1919. This amendment guaranteed women the right to vote and doubled the number of eligible voters.

Besides the vote, women won new opportunities in a number of other areas. More colleges were accepting women as students. Professions such as medicine and law were beginning to open up to women. By 1900, 1,000 female lawyers and 7,000 female doctors were in practice. Women were entering the sciences, too.

Women also took part in the reform movement. Women were leaders in the temperance movement, fighting against alcohol abuse and calling for the government to enact **prohibition**, or a ban on the manufacture and sale of alcoholic beverages. Many wives and mothers believed that alcohol abuse was a threat to their families. In 1917, Congress passed the Eighteenth Amendment, which made the sale of alcoholic drinks illegal.

In the late 1800s and early 1900s, life for African Americans remained difficult. In the South, segregation was a way of life. In both the North and South, African Americans faced discrimination. Discrimination kept them from getting jobs with good pay or from buying or renting homes in white neighborhoods. When whites lost their jobs, some took out their anger on African Americans. In the 1890s, angry mobs **lynched**, or murdered, more than 1,000 African Americans. In general, white Progressives had little concern for people who weren't white. African Americans and other minorities had to fight for justice themselves.

(Continues on the next page.)

Lesson Vocabulary

picket a group of people who are marching in a row to protest something

suffragist a person who worked for women's right to vote

prohibition the legal ban on the manufacture, sale, and transportation of liquor anywhere in the United States from 1920

lynch a mob illegally seizing and killing someone

TOPIC 11 LESSON 5

Lesson Summary
PROGRESS AND SETBACKS FOR JUSTICE

(Continued from page 142)

African American leaders had different ideas about how to fight discrimination. Booker T. Washington urged African Americans to learn trades and earn money. Equality, he believed, would come later. In the meantime, he accepted segregation. Other leaders, such as W.E.B. Du Bois, disagreed. Du Bois believed African Americans should insist immediately on their rights. Du Bois and others founded the NAACP, or the National Association for the Advancement of Colored People, in 1909.

Other groups faced challenges in the early 1900s. Thousands of Mexicans had moved north to the American Southwest. They lived in neighborhoods called **barrios**. They found jobs harvesting crops and building roads. The West Coast became home to many immigrants from Asian countries. Asian workers were paid less than whites and denied promotion to skilled jobs. Still, many white farmers and factory workers resented the success of Japanese immigrants. In 1906, San Francisco forced all Asian students to attend segregated schools. President Roosevelt then arranged the so-called Gentlemen's Agreement with Japan that allowed Japanese women to join their husbands already in the country but banned further immigration. Discrimination persisted, however, as evidenced by a 1913 California law that prohibited Asian non-citizens from owning land. Immigrants from Mexico and Asia sometimes faced violence in the United States. Native Americans continued to face pressure to abandon their reservations and assimilate, while their children were sent to schools where they were given new names, forced to give up their native languages, and forced to adopt white American customs.

Lesson Vocabulary
barrio a Mexican neighborhood in the United States

© Pearson Education, Inc., publishing as Pearson Prentice Hall. All rights reserved.

TOPIC 11 LESSON 6

Lesson Summary
A CHANGING AMERICAN CULTURE

MODIFIED CORNELL NOTES

The population growth of the late 1800s brought great change to the cities of the United States. **Skyscrapers**, new kinds of transportation, and parks were all part of a new look for cities.

A building boom changed the face of American cities. Because cities ran out of space in their downtown areas, builders decided to build tall skyscrapers. The development of electric streetcars relieved traffic on city streets. Public parks were built and gave city dwellers a place to enjoy nature. Shoppers could stroll the streets and look at the displays of goods in **department store** windows.

As more people worked in factories and offices, Americans began to think of work and play as separate activities. People felt a greater need to rest and relax. Americans found escape from their factories, stores, and offices in leisure activities. People played and watched sports, such as football, basketball, and especially baseball. People went to **vaudeville** houses, where they saw variety shows featuring comedians, song-and-dance routines, and acrobats. The invention of the phonograph allowed them to listen to new kinds of music, such as ragtime.

As industry grew, the nation needed an educated workforce. States responded by improving their public schools. In the North, **compulsory education** laws required children to attend public school. Some Catholic groups opened their own **parochial**, or church-sponsored, schools because they felt public schools stressed Protestant teachings. By 1900, there were 6,000 public high schools in the country, and more colleges and universities opened. Schools began special programs to educate students for jobs in business and industry.

(Continues on the next page.)

Lesson Vocabulary

skyscraper a tall building with many floors supported by a lightweight steel frame

department store a large retail store offering a variety of goods organized in separate departments

vaudeville a type of variety show made popular in the late 1800s that included comedians, song-and-dance routines, and acrobats

compulsory education the requirement that children attend school to a certain grade or age

parochial connected to a church parish; often used to refer to church-sponsored schools

TOPIC 11 LESSON 6

Lesson Summary
A CHANGING AMERICAN CULTURE

(Continued from page 144)

MODIFIED CORNELL NOTES

As more Americans learned to read, reading habits changed in the late 1800s. Americans read more newspapers, magazines, and books. Many newspapers began to publish with the immigrant audience in mind. They introduced bold headlines, illustrations, and comics. To grab reader attention, they reported on crimes, gossip, and scandals. Critics called this kind of reporting **yellow journalism**. Newspapers also published sections meant to attract female readers. New technologies, such as the mechanical typesetter, made books cheaper. Low-priced magazines and adventure novels, known as **dime novels**, gained many readers.

A new group of American writers appeared in the late 1800s. They were known as **realists** because they attempted to show life as it really was. Stephen Crane wrote about the Civil War and city slums. In the *Adventures of Huckleberry Finn*, Mark Twain captured **local color**—the special features of a region and the way its people spoke. Some American painters such as Winslow Homer and James Whistler were also realists. They, too, showed the reality of modern life in their work.

Lesson Vocabulary

yellow journalism news reporting, often biased or untrue, that relies on sensational stories and headlines

dime novel in the late 1800s, a low-priced paperback, often an adventure story

realist a writer or artist who aims to show life as it really is

local color the speech and habits of a particular region

Answer the questions below using the information in the Lesson Summaries on the previous pages.

Lesson 1: A New Wave of Immigration

1. Contrast How did the "new immigrants" of the late 1800s differ from the "old immigrants" from earlier in the century?

_____

_____

2. Why did nativists oppose immigration?

_____

_____

Lesson 2: Urbanization

3. Identifying Effects How did American cities changes as a result of urbanization?

_____

_____

4. What services did settlement houses provide?

_____

_____

Lesson 3: The Rise of Progressivism

5. Identifying Problems and Solutions What problems did the spoils system create, and what action was taken solve those problems?

_____

_____

6. What measures did Progressives support to give voters more power?

_____

_____

Lesson 4: The Progressive Presidents

7. Summarize What progressive policies did Theodore Roosevelt pursue as president?

_____

_____

TOPIC 11 | **Review Questions** (continued)
THE PROGRESSIVE ERA

8. How did Woodrow Wilson win the election of 1912?

_____

_____

Lesson 5: Progress and Setbacks for Social Justice

9. **Compare and Contrast** How did Booker T. Washington's and W.E.B. Du Bois's views on ending inequality differ?

_____

_____

10. What amendments to the Constitution did women reformers play a major role in securing? Explain the purpose of each.

_____

_____

Lesson 6: A Changing American Culture

11. What forms of leisure activity were popular in the late 1800s and early 1900s?

_____

_____

12. **Identify Causes** Why did education become such an important issue in the late 1880s?

_____

_____

_____

TOPIC
12

Note Taking Study Guide

IMPERIALISM AND WORLD WAR I

Focus Question: As the United States expanded at home, it also acquired new territories overseas and became more involved in foreign affairs. What were the key events in this expansion?

As you read, identify the key events that showed the expansion of the United States territorially and in its increased involvement in world affairs. In addition to identifying the event, explain its significance.

Year	Events	Significance
1854		
1867		
1890s		
1898		
1899		
1900		
1900		
1903		
1904		
1915		
1916		
1917		
1918		
1919		

TOPIC 12 LESSON 1

Lesson Summary

EXPANSION IN THE PACIFIC

The policy of **isolationism**, or staying out of world affairs, had been maintained for over one hundred years since the founding of the American republic. However, during that time the American republic had also followed a policy of **expansionism**, leading to the extension of the nation's boundaries.

By the late 1800s, the United States was becoming one of the most powerful countries in the world. As American interest in Asia and the Pacific grew, the United States signed treaties with Japan and Russia that benefited the American economy by expanding trade and adding territory rich with natural resources. Japan was closed to foreign trade when American warships landed there in 1853. Impressed by American strength, the Japanese signed the Treaty of Kanagawa, which opened two ports to trade with the United States. In 1867, the United States bought the huge and valuable territory of Alaska from Russia. In that same year, it also **annexed**, or took over, Midway Island, in the middle of the Pacific Ocean.

In the late 1800s, some Americans argued that the United States should adopt a policy of **imperialism**. Supporters of imperialism, or expansionists, argued that the United States needed new markets for foreign trade. They also argued that Americans should bring western culture to the other peoples of the world. In addition, they pointed out that the United States no longer had a western frontier. They said that the country's growing population needed new lands to settle. Congress felt that, in order to accomplish these goals, the United States needed a larger, modernized navy. By 1900, the United States had built a fleet of steam-powered warships known as the Great White Fleet.

As a result of expansionist arguments, the government took action. The United States annexed Hawaii and gained territory in Samoa in the 1890s. In China, the United States competed with other imperialist nations to gain trade. In 1899, the United States persuaded other nations—Britain, France, Germany, Russia, and Japan—to follow an Open Door Policy in China. These nations had carved out spheres of influence—areas where they had special trading privileges and the power to make laws governing its own citizens there—in China. Persuading these nations to follow an Open Door Policy meant that the countries would not stop the United States from trading in China. American foreign trade continued to grow.

Lesson Vocabulary

isolationism a policy of staying out of world affairs

expansionism a policy of extending a nation's boundaries

annex to add on or take over

imperialism a policy of powerful countries seeking to control the economic and political affairs of weaker countries or regions

TOPIC 12 LESSON 2

Lesson Summary
WAR AND EMPIRE

MODIFIED CORNELL NOTES

In 1898, the United States and Spain fought the Spanish-American War. The war had several causes. Cuba, one of the last Spanish colonies in the Western Hemisphere, rebelled against Spain. In response, Spain implemented the **reconcentration** policy, which sent Cubans to detention camps so they could not assist the rebels. Over 100,000 Cubans died in these camps from starvation or disease.

Many Americans wanted to support Cuban independence. Some American newspaper publishers also wanted war, thinking that it would help sell newspapers. They printed stories about cruel Spanish treatment of Cubans that were not always true. Known as yellow journalism, this method of reporting relied on **sensational** stories and headlines to sell newspapers. Finally, the United States battleship *Maine* sunk after an explosion in a Cuban harbor. The cause of the explosion remains a mystery, but many Americans suspected that it was caused by Spain. Although President McKinley initially tried to avoid war by encouraging Spain to negotiate with the rebels, he supported Congress's declaration of war on Spain in April 1898.

The war lasted only four months. American ships quickly defeated the Spanish navy in the Philippines, a major Spanish colony. In Cuba, Theodore Roosevelt led the First Volunteer Cavalry Regiment—later called the Rough Riders—to victory during the fight for the city of Santiago. American ships also destroyed the Spanish fleet in the waters off Cuba. In August, Spain and the United States agreed to end the fighting.

The war had important results. Under the treaty, Cuba became independent of Spain, but it did not have full independence. American troops remained in Cuba. Spain also gave the United States Puerto Rico in the Caribbean and Guam in the Pacific, and the United States purchased the Philippines. Although some Americans felt the treaty violated American principles of democracy by turning the nation into a colonial power, Congress narrowly approved the treaty in 1899. This meant the United States had acquired a true overseas empire.

(Continues on the next page.)

Lesson Vocabulary

reconcentration a policy of moving large numbers of people into camps for political or military purposes

sensational provoking excitement due to something shocking

Lesson Summary
WAR AND EMPIRE

(Continued from page 150)

The United States also forced Cuba to accept the Platt Amendment, which gave the United States the right to **intervene** in Cuba and control of the naval base at Guantanamo Bay. In effect, the amendment made Cuba an American **protectorate**, or nation whose independence is limited by the control of a more powerful country.

The United States set up a new government in Puerto Rico under the Foraker Act of 1900, and made Puerto Ricans citizens of the United States in 1917. However, when the United States took over land in the Philippines after the war ended, Filipinos felt betrayed. The Philippine-American War broke out and lasted until 1902. The United States set up a government in the Philippines similar to the one in Puerto Rico, but did not grant Filipinos citizenship.

Lesson Vocabulary

intervene to get involved in something to influence or change the outcome

protectorate a nation whose independence is limited by the control of a more powerful country

TOPIC
12
LESSON 3

Lesson Summary

U.S. POWER IN LATIN AMERICA

MODIFIED CORNELL NOTES

In the early 1900s, the United States increased its involvement in the affairs of Latin America. One example was the building of the Panama Canal. President Theodore Roosevelt wanted to build a canal across the Isthmus of Panama. An **isthmus** is a narrow strip of land with water on both sides that connects two larger bodies of land. This canal would allow ships to cross from the Atlantic Ocean to the Pacific Ocean much more quickly. Until this time, ships had to sail around South America in order to get from New York to San Francisco. Colombia rejected Roosevelt's plan to rent land in Panama for the canal. However, some people in Panama wanted to secede from Colombia. Roosevelt supported their rebellion. In 1903, the new independent government of Panama allowed the United States to build a canal.

Construction of the canal was slow at first. Workers labored in a tropical environment where mosquitoes carried malaria and yellow fever. Workers took measures to reduce the mosquito population, which dramatically reduced the threat of disease by 1906. More than 40,000 workers removed over 200 million cubic yards of earth and built locks that would be used to raise and lower ships as they passed through the canal. Canal builders completed the canal in 1914. American merchants benefited because they could now ship goods more cheaply to South America and Asia.

Ever since the Monroe Doctrine, the United States had shown a strong interest in the countries of Latin America. In 1904, Roosevelt declared that the United States had the right to use military force to keep order and to protect its interests in Latin America. This **corollary**, or addition, to the Monroe Doctrine was called the Roosevelt Corollary.

(Continues on the next page.)

Lesson Vocabulary

isthmus a narrow strip of land that has water at each side with the strip of land connecting two larger bodies of land

corollary an addition to an earlier stated principle

Name_____ Class_____ Date_____

12 Lesson Summary
LESSON 3 **U.S. POWER IN LATIN AMERICA**

(Continued from page 152)

After Roosevelt, other presidents formed policies to control events in Latin American countries. President William Howard Taft's policy—known as **dollar diplomacy**—called for substituting "dollars for bullets" in an attempt to strengthen economic ties between the United States and Latin America. After Taft, President Woodrow Wilson promoted **moral diplomacy**, which condemned imperialism and promoted the spread of democracy and peace.

However, Roosevelt's "Big Stick" policy remained influential in the way Wilson responded to developments in Latin America in the early 1900s. He sent American troops to intervene in Haiti in 1915 and in the Dominican Republic in 1916. He also sent troops into Mexico in 1916 to support the Mexican government in a civil war. The use of force angered many Latin Americans. Their leaders criticized the United States for interfering in the affairs of other countries. As the United States became increasingly involved in international affairs it became more difficult to stay out of the conflict in Europe, which had begun in 1914.

Lesson Vocabulary

dollar diplomacy President Taft's policy of building strong economic ties to Latin America

moral diplomacy President Wilson's policy of condemning imperialism, spreading democracy, and promoting peace

© Pearson Education, Inc., publishing as Pearson Prentice Hall. All rights reserved.
153

TOPIC 12 LESSON 4

Lesson Summary

A EUROPEAN WAR

In the early 1900s, tensions were high in Europe. Extreme feelings of **nationalism**—a feeling of pride in one's nation—had created mistrust among European nations. Competition among imperialist nations for colonies added to the tension. **Militarism**—a policy of building up strong armed forces to prepare for war—also caused tension. Nations raced against each other to build larger armies and navies. The alliance system was another danger. Allies agreed to support one another in case of attack. Thus, a dispute between two countries could expand to include the allies of each country.

World War I began in 1914 when Franz Ferdinand, a prince of Austria-Hungary, was killed in Bosnia by a member of the Serbian **terrorist** group the Black Hand. Angry that Bosnia remained under AustroHungarian rule, a Serbian nationalist shot the prince. Austria-Hungary responded by declaring war on Serbia. Russia decided to protect Serbia, its ally. Germany, an ally of Austria-Hungary, also entered the war. Before long, the alliance system had drawn all the powerful countries of Europe into the struggle. War raged between the Central Powers—Germany, Austria-Hungary, Bulgaria, and the Ottoman Empire—and the Allied Powers—France, Britain, and Russia. Soon, the armies on both sides dug and lived in trenches. For three years, troops fought bloody battles over a few yards of land that lay between their trenches. Opposing sides shelled and then charged enemy trenches in what is known as **trench warfare**. As neither side was strong enough to defeat the other, a **stalemate** occurred.

When war broke out, the United States remained **neutral**. Still, the war affected the United States. Orders for war goods from Europe strengthened the American economy. However, German U-boat submarines attacked neutral ships, including American ships that traded with Germany's enemies. When the United States threatened to join the Allies, Germany agreed to stop attacking neutral ships without warning.

Lesson Vocabulary

nationalism a devotion to one's nation and its interests

militarism the policy of building up strong armed forces to prepare for war

terrorist one who deliberately uses violence to spread fear and achieve political goals

trench warfare war combat in which soldiers are located in trenches dug into the ground

stalemate a deadlock in which neither side is strong enough to defeat the other

neutral not taking sides in a conflict

TOPIC 12 LESSON 5

Lesson Summary
ENTERING THE WAR

As World War I continued, Americans debated entering the war. Although many Americans wanted to support the Allied Powers, some did not want to declare war on Germany. President Wilson even tried to bring both sides to peace talks. However, recognizing that the United States might still be drawn into the war, Wilson lobbied for a stronger army and navy.

By 1917, a number of factors pushed the United States toward war. Germany started attacking neutral ships again, including several American merchant ships. It also sent a secret note, the Zimmermann telegram, to Mexico, asking Mexico to attack the United States if the United States declared war on Germany. In return, Germany would help Mexico win back territory it had lost to the United States. News of this telegram outraged many Americans. In Russia, a revolution had overthrown the czar, or emperor. With Russia leaning toward democracy, it became easier for Wilson to support the Allies. President Wilson told Congress that the war would make the world "safe for democracy." In April 1917, Congress declared war.

The United States organized for the war effort. To build an army, Congress passed the Selective Service Act. This allowed the government to start a draft, which required people of a certain age to serve in the military. Within the next 18 months, 4 million men and women joined the armed forces.

The government also set up large bureaucracies, or systems of managing government through departments. For example, the Food Administration was responsible for boosting food production. To provide the military with supplies, President Wilson set up the War Industries Board. Government also regulated the use of limited resources and decided what prices to set. As wartime industries grew, the need for workers increased. Women joined the workforce. Many African Americans left the South to find jobs in northern cities and factories. Many were met with discrimination and violence. In the Southwest, almost 100,000 Mexican workers contributed to the war effort.

(Continues on the next page.)

Lesson Vocabulary

czar a Russian emperor

draft a law that requires people of a certain age to perform military service

bureaucracy a system of managing government through departments run by appointed officials

TOPIC 12 LESSON 5

Lesson Summary
ENTERING THE WAR

(Continued from page 155)

In order to help finance and rally public support for the war, the government sold Liberty Bonds to American citizens, raising approximately half of what the United States spent on the war. It also sent out 75,000 men known as "Four-Minute Men," who spoke to the American public about the need to make sacrifices for the goals of freedom and democracy.

Some Americans, known as **pacifists**, opposed the war because they believed war was evil. Other groups, such as Socialists, who believe that people as a whole rather than private individuals should own all property and share profits from business activity, as well as radical labor groups, also opposed the war. The government moved to silence these critics. Congress passed a law making it a crime to criticize the government or interfere with the war effort.

Lesson Vocabulary

pacifist a person who objects to any war; believes war is evil

TOPIC 12 LESSON 6 — Lesson Summary
WINNING THE WAR

MODIFIED CORNELL NOTES

By 1917, the Allies faced hard times. Their armies had suffered millions of casualties. The troops in the field were exhausted and ill. In late 1917, a group led by Vladimir Lenin—who believed in communism—seized power in Russia. This new government decided to withdraw from the war. By early 1918, Russia signed a separate peace treaty—the Treaty of Brest-Litovsk—with Germany. The Allies saw the treaty as a betrayal. The treaty hurt the Allies because Germany could now concentrate on fighting the other Allies. By mid-1918, German forces had advanced to only 50 miles outside of Paris.

American soldiers, however, helped change the course of the war. By June 1918, the American Expeditionary Forces were arriving in Europe in huge numbers. American soldiers were fresh and ready for battle. They helped fight a series of battles that slowly pushed Germany out of the territory it had captured. The Battle of the Argonne Forest in the autumn of 1918 lasted for 47 days. More than a million Americans took part in the battle. Finally, the Allies smashed through the German defense.

Germany could fight no longer and called on President Wilson to arrange an **armistice**, or agreement to stop fighting, in October 1918. As part of this agreement, Wilson demanded that the German emperor **abdicate**, or give up power. Germany agreed to the armistice in November 1918. The costs of the war were huge. Much of northern France lay in ruins. Between 8 and 9 million people died in battle and more than 20 million soldiers were wounded. This was more people than had died in all the wars fought over the previous 100 years. The United States lost over 100,000 men.

Much of Europe lay in ruins. Millions of Germans faced starvation and many children throughout Europe were left orphaned and homeless. Then, from 1918 to 1919, an outbreak of **influenza**— an infection of the respiratory tract marked by fever, chills, and weakness—spread across the globe. It quickly became an **epidemic**, or contagious disease that spreads rapidly among large numbers of people, killing over 30 million worldwide.

Lesson Vocabulary

armistice an agreement to stop fighting

abdicate to give up power

influenza an infection of the respiratory tract that is marked by fever, chills, and a general feeling of weakness

epidemic the rapid spread of contagious disease

TOPIC 12
LESSON 7

Lesson Summary
WILSON AND ISOLATIONISM

In 1918, President Woodrow Wilson proposed a plan to bring peace to Europe. Wilson's fourteen-point peace plan contained a number of important ideas. One idea was the principle of **self-determination**, or the right for nations to have their own territory and forms of government. The most important part of the plan was Wilson's idea of an association of nations. The association, called the League of Nations, would work to bring about world peace and cooperation.

The Big Four—leaders of Britain, France, the United States, and Italy—disagreed on what the goals of peace negotiations in Paris should be. Wilson's goals were different from those of the other Allied leaders. Wilson wanted a "peace without victory" in which the defeated countries would not be punished. He hoped to build good relations between countries in order to prevent further wars. The other Allies, however, wanted mainly to punish Germany. They insisted that Germany pay **reparations**, or cash payments, for the losses the Allies had suffered during the war.

By June 1919, the Allied Powers had reached an agreement called the Treaty of Versailles. The treaty included some of Wilson's ideas, such as the League of Nations. However, it also included many measures that were harsh on Germany. For example, Germany had to pay huge reparations. It also lost its colonies, which were put under the control of other nations.

Meanwhile, Britain and France were given **mandates**, or authorization, by the League of Nations to govern territory in the former Ottoman Empire. In addition, the Allies created the new nations of Czechoslovakia, Yugoslavia, and others out of land formerly ruled by Germany, Russia, and Austria-Hungary. Poland regained its independence.

(Continues on the next page.)

Lesson Vocabulary

self-determination the right of national groups to have their own territory and forms of government

reparation a cash payment made by a defeated nation to a victorious nation to pay for losses suffered during a war

mandate an authorization granted to a member of the League of Nations to govern a former German or Turkish colony

TOPIC 12 LESSON 7 — Lesson Summary
WILSON AND ISOLATIONISM

(Continued from page 158)

In the United States, the treaty had to be approved by the Senate. A number of powerful senators who were **isolationists**—people who wanted the United States to stay out of world affairs—opposed the treaty. They believed that membership in the League of Nations might involve the United States in future European wars. Wilson failed to win support for the treaty. In November 1919, the Senate rejected the Treaty of Versailles. It would not be until 1921 that the United States signed a peace treaty with Germany. Still, many other nations had approved the treaty and joined the League of Nations. However, without the United States' involvement, the League failed to protect its members against aggression.

Lesson Vocabulary

isolationist after World War I, any American who wanted the United States to stay out of world affairs

Name_____ Class_____ Date_____

Review Questions

TOPIC 12

IMPERIALISM AND WORLD WAR I

Answer the questions below using the information in the Lesson Summaries on the previous pages.

Lesson 1: Expansion in the Pacific

1. What new lands did the United States acquire in the second half of the 1800s?

_____

_____

2. Summarize What reasons did expansionists offer for the United States to adopt a policy of imperialism?

_____

_____

Lesson 2: War and Empire

3. Summarize What events led the United States to go to war with Spain?

_____

_____

4. What new territories did the United States acquire as a result of the Spanish-American War?

_____

_____

Lesson 3: U.S. Power in Latin America

5. Why did Roosevelt want to build the Panama Canal?

_____

_____

6. Compare and Contrast What common goal did the Latin American policies of President Theodore Roosevelt, President Taft, and President Wilson share, and how did their policies differ?

_____

_____

TOPIC 12 **Review Questions** (continued)
IMPERIALISM AND WORLD WAR I

Lesson 4: A European War

7. What event sparked World War I on June 28, 1914?

_____

_____

8. **Summarize** How did the alliance system draw all the powerful countries into war?

_____

_____

Lesson 5: Entering the War

9. What three factors pushed the United States toward war?

_____

_____

10. **Summarize** Once the United States entered the war, what steps did the U.S. government take to organize the war effort?

_____

_____

Lesson 6: Winning the War

11. **Identifying Effect** What was the effect of Russia's decision to withdraw from World War I?

_____

_____

12. **Identifying Effect** How did the arrival of United States troops affect the course of the war?

_____

_____

TOPIC 12 Review Questions (continued)
IMPERIALISM AND WORLD WAR I

Lesson 7: Wilson and Isolationism

13. What were two key ideas in Wilson's fourteen-point plan?

_____

_____

14. Identify Main Ideas Why did isolationists oppose the Treaty of Versailles?

_____

_____

Note Taking Study Guide
PROSPERITY AND DEPRESSION

Focus Question: The United States saw periods of great prosperity in the Roaring Twenties and economic distress in the Great Depression. What were the key features of American political, economic, social, and cultural life in these periods?

As you read, think about the most important features of American life in each of the four categories in the two periods and record your ideas.

Roaring Twenties	Great Depression
Political:	**Political:**
Economic:	**Economic:**
Social:	**Social:**
Cultural:	**Cultural:**

TOPIC 13 LESSON 1

Lesson Summary
HARDING AND COOLIDGE

After World War I, soldiers coming home from the war began to look for jobs. At the same time, however, factories stopped turning out war materials. Fewer jobs were available. As a result, the American economy suffered a **recession**, or economic downturn. In the 1920 election, a Republican, Warren G. Harding, was elected President. Voters hoped that he would improve the economy. However, Harding was faced with a series of political scandals such as the Teapot Dome Scandal. Some of the people he appointed to office used their government jobs to enrich themselves. When Harding died of a heart attack in 1923, Vice President Calvin Coolidge became President.

Coolidge believed that the prosperity of all Americans depended on the prosperity of American businesses. Under his pro-business policies, the American economy had a period of rapid growth. Credit became increasingly available to consumers as businesses offered **installment buying** programs to consumers—allowing consumers to pay off purchases in easy payments, or installments—that fueled a rapid expansion of credit and consumption. More people bought stock, or shares of ownership, in corporations than ever before. Demand for stock drove stock prices up. However, a few experts warned that stock market rise could not last forever.

During this period, the United States pursued a policy of isolationism, or limiting its role in foreign affairs. However, the United States intervened to protect its economic interests in Latin America. It refused to recognize the Soviet Union, where the government was based on **communism**, or communist party control of government and the economy. The United States also joined other nations in supporting **disarmament**, or the reduction of armed forces and weapons of war. The United States also pursued efforts to promote international peace. For example, in 1928, 68 nations, including the United States, signed the Kellogg-Briand Pact, which outlawed war.

Lesson Vocabulary

recession an economic slump that is milder than a depression

installment buying buying on credit, with regular payments to cover the full price plus interest

communism an economic system in which all wealth and property are owned by the state

disarmament a reduction of armed forces and weapons of war

Lesson Summary
SOCIAL CHANGE

American society went through dramatic changes in the 1920s. New ideas, new products, and new forms of entertainment changed the American way of life.

One such change began in January 1920, when the Eighteenth Amendment to the Constitution became law. This amendment made it illegal to make or sell alcohol anywhere in the United States. Because it prohibited people from drinking alcohol, the amendment began the period known as Prohibition. Prohibition had long been a goal of reformers, who hoped it would improve American life. In the end, however, it did not work. Many Americans found ways to get alcohol. Prohibition led to an increase in **organized crime**, or criminal activity organized as a business. Criminals provided alcohol to the illegal clubs where it was served. Many Americans came to believe Prohibition had undermined respect for the law. It was **repealed**, or canceled, in 1933.

The Nineteenth Amendment, passed in 1920, brought more changes to American life. It gave women the right to vote. The lives of women were changing in other ways, too. During World War I, thousands of women had begun working outside the home. While many lost their jobs when the troops came home, some remained in the work force. In the home, new appliances such as refrigerators and vacuum cleaners made housework easier.

Other changes occurred in the 1920s. The automobile came into much wider use, allowing people to move more easily from place to place. As a result, **suburbs**, or communities linked to central cities but located outside them, began to grow. A new **mass culture**—a set of values and practices that arise from listening to the same media sources across a nation—arose that crossed state lines. People drove to stores, schools, and work. New types of entertainment, such as radio and movies, became very popular. Hollywood became the movie capital of the world, while millions of Americans attended movies every week.

Lesson Vocabulary

organized crime criminal activity carried on by one or more organized groups as a business

repeal to cancel, remove from law

suburb a residential area on the outskirts of a city

mass culture a set of shared practices and beliefs that arise from widespread exposure to the same media

TOPIC 13 LESSON 3
Lesson Summary
THE ROARING TWENTIES CULTURE

MODIFIED CORNELL NOTES

In the United States, the 1920s became known as the Roaring Twenties. New dances, music, and games swept the country. Americans seemed to "roar" with fun and laughter. A number of **fads**, such as dance contests, flagpole sitting, and styles of dress, came and went.

The 1920s were also called the Jazz Age. **Jazz** was a popular new kind of music created by African American musicians, such as Louis Armstrong. It first developed in New Orleans and then spread around the country. Today, jazz is considered one of the most significant cultural achievements of the United States.

A new generation of American writers gained worldwide fame in the 1920s. Many criticized Americans for caring too much about money and fun. Some of these critics lived as **expatriates**, people who leave their country to live in a foreign land. Ernest Hemingway—a one-time expatriate—drew on his World War I experiences to write about the horrors of war. F. Scott Fitzgerald wrote about wealthy young people who attended countless parties but could not find happiness.

The neighborhood of Harlem in New York City became a center for the arts. There, large numbers of African American musicians, artists, and writers created a movement called the Harlem Renaissance. During the Harlem Renaissance many great works of art were produced. African American writers and artists celebrated their heritage.

Radio, movies, and newspapers created heroes known across the country. Many athletes, such as Babe Ruth, star of the New York Yankees, became famous. The greatest popular hero of the decade was Charles Lindbergh. In 1927, he became the first person to fly nonstop across the Atlantic Ocean alone.

Lesson Vocabulary

fad an activity or fashion that is taken up with great passion for a short time

jazz a music style developed by African Americans in the early 1900s that developed from blues, ragtime, and other earlier styles

expatriate a person who leaves his or her own country and takes up residence in a foreign land

TOPIC 13 LESSON 4

Lesson Summary
DIVISION AND INEQUALITY

Many Americans did not share in the **prosperity** of the 1920s. Railroad workers lost jobs as more people used cars. The power of labor unions decreased as labor organizations formed **company unions**—unions that were controlled by management. Many farmers suffered terribly.

Some Americans believed that too many people were immigrating to the United States. Some believed that immigrants brought political ideas that posed dangers to the American way of life. Some feared that there were enemy spies prepared to carry out **sabotage**, or the secret destruction of property or interference with work, in factories.

A growing tide of **nativism** gripped the nation. This is the belief that the government should limit immigration and favor native-born citizens. Many foreigners were **deported**, or forcibly removed from the country. Congress passed new laws that limited immigration. Under the new **quota system**, only a certain number of people from each country could enter the United States. In the South, a revived Ku Klux Klan terrorized African Americans, immigrants, Catholics, and Jews. Many African Americans migrated to northern cities to take factory jobs and escape racial prejudice.

The government also took harsh actions against communists. During the Red Scare, suspected communists were arrested.

In 1925, a legal case known as the Scopes Trial captured the nation's attention. Two of the best lawyers in the country argued for or against the teaching of evolution in schools. The side for teaching evolution lost.

Three years later, in 1928, voters had to choose between two presidential candidates: the Republican, Herbert Hoover, a prosperous businessman; and the Democrat, Alfred E. Smith, the son of Irish immigrants. Hoover won the presidency on the issues of prosperity and Prohibition.

Lesson Vocabulary

company union a labor organization limited to a single company that is controlled by management

sabotage the secret destruction of property or interference with production

nativism the belief that native-born citizens' interests should be protected, usually involving hostility toward foreigners and immigration

deport to forcibly remove from a country

quota system a system that limits the number of certain kinds of people admitted to an institution or country; beginning in the 1920s, a system that allowed only a certain number of people from each country to immigrate to the United States

Lesson Summary
ENTERING THE GREAT DEPRESSION

MODIFIED CORNELL NOTES

By the end of the 1920s there were signs that the economy was failing. However, most Americans were not aware of any problems. Then, in 1929, there was a crash, or a severe fall in prices, in the stock market. It began when a few investors sold stocks because they thought that the prosperity of the 1920s might be over. As prices began to drop, more people began selling their stocks, and stock prices fell further. Soon people panicked and tried to sell before prices fell even further. So many people lost their fortunes on October 29 that it was called Black Tuesday.

The stock market crash marked the beginning of a period of economic hard times known as the Great Depression. This period lasted until 1941. Factories cut back on production and laid off workers. Many businesses declared that they were **bankrupt**, or unable to pay their bills and other debts. The unemployment rate rose very high. Many Americans had no money to buy food or pay rent. The economic pressures caused many families to split up and forced young children to work.

President Herbert Hoover responded cautiously. He did not believe that the government should help businesses directly. At first, he tried to restore confidence by predicting better times. When the hard times continued, Hoover took other steps. He set up **public works** programs—projects built by the government for public use—and **relief programs**, such as **soup kitchens**, to help the needy. Still, the Depression deepened. Hoovervilles across the nation housed clusters of homeless people in poorly built shanties on vacant land. When the Bonus Army, a group of World War I veterans demanding early payment of a promised **bonus**, camped in a tent city in Washington, D.C., Hoover used the army to force veterans to leave. Many people were shocked by the use of force. By 1932, Americans wanted a new leader.

Lesson Vocabulary
bankrupt unable to pay debts

public works the construction of government-funded public buildings, roads, dams, and other public structures

relief program a government program to help the needy

soup kitchens a place where food is provided to the needy at little or no charge

bonus an additional sum of money

Lesson Summary
ROOSEVELT'S NEW DEAL

In 1932, Franklin Delano Roosevelt, known as FDR, was elected president. During the campaign, FDR promised to help the unemployed, farmers, and the elderly. Many Americans believed that he would take action to improve the economy.

Once in office, Roosevelt first acted to help the banks. The Depression had caused many banks to close because they had lent out money that could not be paid back. People lost the money they had deposited in those banks. Many depositors became afraid and took their savings out of other banks. FDR knew that the economy would not recover without strong banks able to make loans. First, he declared a **bank holiday**, closing every bank in the country for four days. Urged by the president, Congress passed laws, such as the Emergency Banking Relief Act, that strengthened the banking system. Roosevelt gave a speech on the radio, called a **fireside chat**, to explain that the banks were now safe. Depositors returned their money to the banks, and the American banking system regained strength.

The bank bill was the first of many bills FDR sent to Congress during the first three months he was in office. Congress quickly passed many of these. This period was called the Hundred Days. Roosevelt called his plan for economic recovery the New Deal. The New Deal had three main goals: relief for the unemployed, plans for recovery, and reforms to prevent another depression. The government began large public works programs, such as the Civilian Conservation Corps, to provide people with jobs. Other laws helped raise the prices of agricultural products.

Government and industry agreed on new rules for doing business. The National Recovery Act gave the National Recovery Administration authority to set standards for production, wages, prices, and working conditions. Congress passed laws to regulate the stock market. Congress also created the Tennessee Valley Authority, which helped control flooding in the Southeast and provide electricity to residents.

(Continues on the next page.)

Lesson Vocabulary

bank holiday one or more weekdays when banks are closed; during the Great Depression, a four-day period when the federal government ordered banks closed

fireside chat a radio speech given by President Franklin D. Roosevelt while in office

Name_____ Class_____ Date_____

MODIFIED CORNELL NOTES

(Continued from page 169)

The first hundred days of the New Deal made Americans feel hopeful. Still, the Depression continued. Criticism of FDR and his policies grew. Some people wanted the government to do more to help people. Others did not want the government to expand its power. They argued that the New Deal was interfering too much with business and with people's lives. New Deal critics thought that they could end the Depression by increasing taxes or by insisting that people over age sixty retire.

The Supreme Court ruled that many New Deal laws were unconstitutional. Roosevelt wanted to appoint more judges who supported his programs. Many Americans feared that his plan to "pack" the Supreme Court would destroy the balance of powers. FDR withdrew his proposal. Roosevelt continued to expand the New Deal by passing new laws that worked around the Supreme Court's objections. In 1935, Congress passed the Social Security Act. This act provided **pensions**—sums of money paid to people during retirement—for older people. It also set up a system through which unemployed people were given small payments until they found work, and states were given money to support dependent children and people with disabilities. Roosevelt also pushed for laws strengthening labor unions. The National Labor Relations Act protected workers from hostile management practices. Workers were given more power to negotiate with their employers.

The debate for and against the New Deal has continued to this day. Whether good or bad, the New Deal was a turning point in American history. For the first time, large numbers of people had direct contact with the federal government. New Deal programs such as Social Security have affected the lives of almost every American citizen.

Lesson Vocabulary

pension a sum of money paid to people on a regular basis after they retire

Lesson Summary
LIFE DURING THE GREAT DEPRESSION

Drought hit the western Great Plains states. This area, which included parts of Texas, Oklahoma, and Arkansas, became known as the Dust Bowl. The **topsoil** became so dry that winds blew it away in blinding dust storms. Farming was nearly impossible. Many farmers left and traveled west to become **migrant workers**—people who move from one region to another in search of work—on the West Coast. There, new hardships awaited them. Those who were able to find work were paid very little. Many lived in tents and shacks without water or electricity.

Women, African Americans, and other minority groups faced hardships during the Depression. Women and minorities were usually the first to lose jobs. Then, when jobs became available, white men were hired back first. First Lady Eleanor Roosevelt spoke out in support of women's rights. Despite setbacks, under the New Deal thousands of young African American men learned trades. President Roosevelt also appointed black leaders to advisory positions within the White House—who became known as the Black Cabinet. President Roosevelt also encouraged new policies toward Native Americans. Known as the Indian New Deal, these policies gave Indian nations greater control over their own affairs.

Americans found ways to take their minds off the Depression. Every night, millions of people tuned in to the radio. They also went to the movies to watch stories about happy families and people finding love and success. The radio and the movies helped people forget about their troubles at least for a little while. Some American artists used the Depression as a backdrop for their art. Writer John Steinbeck's novel *The Grapes of Wrath* tells the story of a migrant family. Photographers like Dorothea Lange captured images of that time in their work.

Lesson Vocabulary

topsoil the upper part of the soil that nourishes plants' roots

migrant workers a person who moves from one region to another in search of work

Name_____ Class_____ Date_____

Answer the questions below using the information in the Lesson Summaries on the previous pages.

Lesson 1: Harding and Coolidge

1. **Draw Conclusions** How were disarmament and the Kellogg-Briand Pact consistent with a policy of isolationism?

_____

_____

2. What role did credit play in the growth of the American economy in the 1920s?

_____

_____

Lesson 2: Social Change

3. **Identify Main Ideas** Why was the Eighteenth Amendment repealed?

_____

_____

4. Name two examples of mass culture that developed in the 1920s.

_____

_____

Lesson 3: Roaring Twenties Culture

5. What African American artistic and literary movement was prominent in the 1920s?

_____

_____

6. **Sequence** Trace the development and spread of jazz.

_____

_____

Lesson 4: Division and Inequality

7. **Identify Effects** What did the growing tide of nativism that gripped the country lead to?

_____

_____

8. What was the Red Scare?

_____

_____

Review Questions (continued)
PROSPERITY AND DEPRESSION

Lesson 5: Entering the Great Depression

9. Identify Supporting Details What were some of the economic conditions that characterized the Great Depression?

_____

_____

10. Name two measures President Hoover took in response to the Great Depression.

_____

_____

Lesson 6: Roosevelt's New Deal

11. What were the three main goals of the New Deal?

_____

_____

12. Identify Supporting Details Name two New Deal laws and describe what each did.

_____

_____

Lesson 7: Life During the Great Depression

13. What was the so-called "Black Cabinet"?

_____

_____

14. Identify Main Ideas and Details What was the Dust Bowl, and what effect did it have on people who experienced it?

_____

_____

TOPIC 14

Note Taking Study Guide

WORLD WAR II

Focus Question: The United States faced enormous challenges in World War II. What important events and trends are associated with the years before and during that conflict?

As you read, focus upon the major causes of World War II, the most important events of that war, and the developments that arose from it. Record those causes, events, and developments.

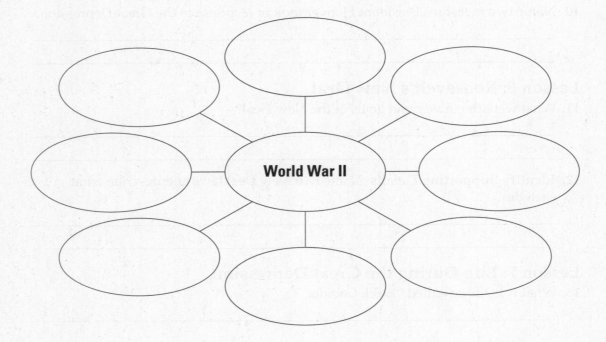

Lesson Summary
AGGRESSION OVERSEAS AND ISOLATIONISM AT HOME

During the 1920s and 1930s, dictators came to power in various countries around the world. Dictators in Germany and Italy were **fascists** who promoted militarism, extreme nationalism, and unquestioned loyalty to the state. Germany, Italy, and the Soviet Union set up **totalitarian states**, where a single party controls the government and every aspect of peoples' lives. In these states, criticism of the government is severely punished.

Joseph Stalin was the dictator of the Soviet Union. Brutal measures were used to modernize the country's industry and agriculture. Peasants were forced to hand over their land to government-run farms. People who resisted were executed or sent to labor camps.

Benito Mussolini and his Fascist party seized power in Italy in 1922. Mussolini outlawed all political parties except his own. Many Italians were bitter over the Treaty of Versailles, which they felt did not grant Italy the territory it wanted. Mussolini embarked on a program of military **aggression**, or warlike acts by one country against another without just cause. Italy invaded Ethiopia in 1935.

Adolf Hitler and his Nazi party seized power in Germany in 1933. Germans were bitter about being blamed for World War I and for bearing the heavy costs of war reparations. Hitler's **scapegoats** were primarily Jews and other "traitors" whom he blamed for Germany's troubles. As his power grew, thousands of Jews were sent to **concentration camps**, or prison camps for civilians who are considered enemies of the state.

In Japan, military leaders seized power. In the early 1930s, hungry for natural resources such as coal and iron, Japan invaded China. During the 1930s, Italy, Germany, and Japan committed acts of aggression that threatened world peace. Events were driving the world to another war.

(Continues on the next page.)

Lesson Vocabulary

Fascism a political system that is rooted in militarism, extreme nationalism, and blind loyalty to the state

totalitarian state a country where a single party controls the government and every aspect of people's lives

aggression a warlike act by one country without just cause

scapegoat a person or group who is made to bear the blame for others

concentration camp a prison camp for civilians who are considered enemies of the state

TOPIC 14 LESSON 1 — Lesson Summary

AGGRESSION OVERSEAS AND ISOLATIONISM AT HOME

MODIFIED CORNELL NOTES

(Continued from page 175)

In the United States, people continued to struggle through the Great Depression. Few wanted to get involved in another war. Throughout most of the 1930s, the country remained officially neutral in the growing conflicts of Europe and Asia. In 1935, Congress passed the first of a series of Neutrality Acts. These acts banned arms sales or loans to countries at war. As part of his Good Neighbor Policy, President Franklin Roosevelt sought to improve relations with Latin America by withdrawing American troops from Nicaragua and Haiti. However, in 1933, he restored diplomatic relations with the Soviet Union in an attempt to limit Japanese expansion in Asia.

MODIFIED CORNELL NOTES

During the late 1930s, Italy, Japan, and Germany continued their aggression. The United States and the European democracies did little in response.

In 1937, Japan began an all-out war against China. It also threatened the Philippines, which the United States controlled. American leaders did not take a strong stand despite concerns over Japanese treatment of Chinese civilians and the possibility of reduced access to trade in China.

In 1938, Hitler annexed Austria. Then he claimed part of Czechoslovakia. Britain and France were eager to avoid war. At the Munich Conference in 1938, they pursued a policy of **appeasement**, the practice of giving in to aggression in order to avoid war. Western leaders made a deal that Germany could keep this land if no additional attempts to expand were made. However, this policy of appeasement failed. Germany seized the rest of Czechoslovakia. Then, in August 1939, Hitler signed the Nazi-Soviet Pact with Joseph Stalin, the leader of the Soviet Union. Both countries agreed not to attack one another and to divide Poland as well as other parts of Eastern Europe. Germany launched a **blitzkrieg**, or lightning war, against Poland in September 1939. As a result, Great Britain and France declared war on Germany.

World War II had begun. By the summer of 1940, German forces had conquered France and were threatening Britain. However, Hitler gave up on plans to invade Britain after it successfully defended itself from air attacks during the Battle of Britain.

When war broke out in Europe, the United States declared that it would remain neutral. President Roosevelt, like most Americans, sympathized with Britain and France. He created programs by which the United States supplied planes, guns, and other supplies to Britain. For example, Congress passed the Lend-Lease Act in 1941, allowing for sales or loans of war materials to "any country whose defense the President deems vital to the defense of the United States." This program was **extended** to the Soviet Union after Hitler invaded it in 1941. Roosevelt quietly began preparing the nation for war.

(Continues on the next page.)

Lesson Vocabulary

appeasement the practice of giving in to aggression in order to avoid war

blitzkrieg the swift and powerful German military attacks in World War II; "lightning war"

extend to make larger in impact or meaning

<table>
<tr><td>TOPIC
14
LESSON 2</td><td>**Lesson Summary**
ENTERING WORLD WAR II</td></tr>
</table>

MODIFIED CORNELL NOTES

(Continued from page 177)

Tensions between the United States and Japan grew. The United States refused to sell oil and metal to Japan unless it stopped its attacks on other countries. On December 7, 1941, Japanese planes made a surprise raid on the American naval base at Pearl Harbor in Hawaii. The attack destroyed many ships and planes. More than 2,400 people died. An outraged Congress declared war on Japan. The United States entered the war on the side of the Allies, which included Britain, France, the Soviet Union, China, and 45 other countries. Italy, Japan, Germany, and six other nations joined to form the Axis powers.

Lesson Summary
THE HOME FRONT

MODIFIED CORNELL NOTES

After the attack on Pearl Harbor, the United States mobilized for war. The military built bases all over the country to train forces for combat. The War Production Board helped factories shift to the production of weapons, ships, and planes. As a result, other goods became scarce. The government **rationed** the amount of certain goods that people could buy. To combat food shortages, many Americans planted **victory gardens**. The war quickly ended the Great Depression. Unemployment fell as millions of jobs opened up in factories.

During the war, more than 6 million women entered the American work force. They replaced men who had joined the armed services. Women also joined the armed forces. While not allowed to fight, women served in other important roles.

Latinos, African Americans, Native Americans, and other minorities contributed to the war effort. Many found jobs in factories. The Bracero Program enabled Mexican laborers to find work in the United States. African Americans pursued a "Double V" campaign, where they hoped to have victory over the enemy abroad and victory over discrimination at home. Minorities also served in the military. Although they were placed in segregated units, African Americans served heroically. For example, the Tuskegee Airmen—a group of African American fighter pilots—destroyed or damaged about 400 enemy aircraft by the end of the war. More than one out of three able-bodied Native American men were in uniform. Thousands of Puerto Ricans and Mexican Americans also served.

Some Americans were treated unjustly during the war. After Pearl Harbor, some Americans questioned the **loyalty** of Japanese Americans. No evidence of disloyalty existed. Yet the government forced about 110,000 Japanese Americans to move to "relocation camps." Still, many Japanese Americans served in the armed forces during the war, most in segregated units that fought in Europe. In 1988, Congress apologized to these Japanese Americans who had suffered from **internment**, or temporary imprisonment. Approximately 11,000 German Americans and hundreds of Italian Americans were also interned in relocation camps during the war.

Lesson Vocabulary

rationing limiting the amount of certain goods that people can buy

victory garden during World War II, a vegetable garden planted to combat food shortages in the United States

loyalty having strong, unwavering support for someone

internment the temporary imprisonment of members of a specific group

TOPIC 14 LESSON 4 — Lesson Summary
WINNING A DEADLY WAR

In early 1942, it seemed likely that the Allies would lose. Hitler was in control of most of Europe and North Africa. His forces were advancing deep into the Soviet Union. Japan was advancing across Asia and the Pacific. The Japanese had captured Guam, Hong Kong, and Singapore and had driven the United States out of the Philippines.

However, later that year, the Allies began to have successes. There were several key turning points in the war. The United States Navy won a major victory at the Battle of Midway in the Pacific. American planes sank four Japanese aircraft carriers. This prevented Japan from attacking Hawaii again. In 1943, Allied troops drove the Germans from North Africa and then invaded Italy. Meanwhile, the Soviets slowly pushed the Germans back west. Finally came D-Day on June 6, 1944. This sea, air, and land invasion was part of Operation Overlord, the code name for the Allied invasion of Europe. The Allies landed an invasion force on the beaches of Normandy in northern France. By August, Allied troops entered Paris.

The invasion force began moving east toward Germany. The Germans mounted a fierce counter-attack in the Battle of the Bulge, but were unable to push the Allied forces back. By 1945, American troops were closing in on Berlin, the German capital, from the west. Soviet troops advanced from the east. Allied air forces pounded the city. Hitler committed suicide rather than surrender, but Germany had lost the war. On May 8, 1945, the Allies celebrated victory in Europe. Sadly, after leading the country through the Great Depression and World War II, President Roosevelt died one month before the Germans surrendered.

However, the war in the Pacific was not over. After the Battle of Midway, the United States fought to take control of the Pacific from Japan. Through a campaign of **island-hopping**, American forces captured islands closer and closer to Japan. American bombers began to shell Japanese factories and cities. Still, the Japanese did not seem ready to surrender. Japanese **kamikaze** pilots ran suicide missions where they deliberately crashed their planes with bombs into Allied ships. Some American officials warned that an invasion of Japan would be long and bloody, leading to as many as 250,000 American casualties.

(Continues on the next page.)

Lesson Vocabulary

island-hopping during World War II, an Allied strategy of capturing Japanese-held islands to gain control of the Pacific

kamikaze a World War II Japanese pilot trained to make a suicidal crash attack, usually upon a ship

TOPIC 14 LESSON 4

Lesson Summary
WINNING A DEADLY WAR

(Continued from page 180)

The Allies had a difficult decision to make. During the war, American scientists developed the atomic bomb. President Harry S. Truman thought that this weapon could finally end the war. In the Potsdam Declaration, Allied leaders warned Japan to surrender or face terrible destruction. The Japanese ignored this message, not knowing about the atomic bomb. In August 1945, an American bomber dropped a single atomic bomb, destroying the Japanese city of Hiroshima and killing at least 70,000 people. After the United States dropped a second bomb on Nagasaki a few days later, Japan finally surrendered.

World War II was the deadliest war in human history. Historians estimate that between 30 and 60 million people were killed. Bombs had destroyed houses, factories, and farms. Japan had brutally mistreated prisoners of war. Especially horrifying was the Holocaust, the slaughter of Europe's Jews by the Nazis. After the full truth of the Holocaust was revealed, some Nazi leaders were charged with war crimes. At the Nuremberg Trials, 12 were sentenced to death. Thousands of other Nazis were imprisoned. Allied war leaders also tried and executed Japanese leaders accused of war crimes.

TOPIC 14 — Review Questions
WORLD WAR II

Answer the questions below using the information in the Lesson Summaries on the previous pages.

Lesson 1: Aggression Overseas and Isolationism at Home

1. Draw Conclusions How did the rise of dictators lead to World War II?

_____

_____

2. Identify Main Idea and Supporting Details How did the United States respond to the growing threat of war in Europe and Asia?

_____

_____

Lesson 2: Entering World War II

3. Contrast the goal and the result of the policy of appeasement of German aggression against Czechoslovakia.

_____

_____

4. How did the United States support the Allies while maintaining official neutrality?

_____

_____

_____

Lesson 3: The Home Front

5. Identify Main Idea and Details What are some ways that ordinary Americans contributed to the war effort on the home front?

_____

_____

6. Give examples of prejudice on the American home front.

_____

_____

Lesson 4: Winning a Deadly War

7. Identify Main Ideas How did the Allies win the war in Europe?

_____

_____

8. Identify Main Ideas How did the Allies win the war in the Pacific?

_____

_____

TOPIC 15 — Note Taking Study Guide
POSTWAR AMERICA

Focus Question: The United States saw many changes from the end of World War II through the early 1970s. What were the most important features of the Cold War and the domestic changes that Americans saw in these decades?

As you read, list the key international events of the Cold War in the first column. Then, in the second column, chart the major developments in U.S. domestic life during the Cold War. A few bullet points have been provided, but you will need to add more.

Cold War	Changes at Home
•	•
•	•
•	•
•	•

Name_____ Class_____ Date_____

Lesson Summary
THE BEGINNING OF THE COLD WAR

MODIFIED CORNELL NOTES

After World War II, the United States and the Soviet Union became rivals. They competed for influence around the world but did not face each other directly in battle. This conflict became known as the Cold War. The United States distrusted the communist government of the Soviet Union, which rejected religion and the idea of private property. The Soviet Union also distrusted the United States, fearing invasion from the West. The distrust between the two sides increased when the Soviet Union did not allow fair elections in the countries it had freed from Germany. By 1948, the countries of Eastern Europe had become **satellite nations** of the Soviet Union. Winston Churchill accused the Soviet Union of having built an **iron curtain**—the zone between Western Europe and Soviet-controlled satellite nations—behind which democracy was not possible and people lived under oppressive governments.

President Truman decided on a policy of **containment**—preventing the spread of Soviet influence beyond where it already existed. Under the Truman Doctrine, the United States helped nations resist communist expansion. Under the Marshall Plan, the United States helped the countries of Western Europe rebuild from war damage. American aid helped prevent communist revolutions in those countries.

American and Soviet actions resulted in many conflicts. In 1948, conflict erupted over the city of Berlin. Soviet leader Joseph Stalin blockaded the entrance to West Berlin—then under the control of Western powers—which prevented American, British, and French aid from reaching the city. President Truman approved the Berlin Airlift, which restored the flow of aid. When the Soviet blockade of West Berlin ended in 1949, the Western powers united their zones into the Federal Republic of Germany, or West Germany.

(Continues on the next page.)

Lesson Vocabulary

satellite nation a nation that is dominated politically and economically by a more powerful nation

iron curtain a term coined by Winston Churchill to describe the border between the Soviet satellite nations and Western Europe

containment the policy of trying to prevent the spread of Soviet influence beyond where it already existed

Name_____ Class_____ Date_____

MODIFIED CORNELL NOTES

(Continued from page 184)

The Soviets became convinced the Western powers were determined to reunite Germany. In addition, what had become East Germany was poor while West Germany was better off, prompting many to cross the border into West Berlin. As a result, in 1961 the Soviets built the Berlin Wall, a large concrete wall topped with barbed wire separating East and West Berlin. It became a symbol of the Cold War. Tensions increased when the Soviet Union tested an atomic bomb and the communists gained power in China.

While the United States and Soviet Union formed new military alliances during the Cold War, they both joined other nations in international alliances whose purpose was to promote stability within the international system. In 1945, fifty-one nations ratified the United Nations **charter**. In 1949, the United States joined with Western European nations to form the North Atlantic Treaty Organization (NATO), whose purpose was to protect member nations in the event of an attack. Six years later, the Soviet Union formed its own defensive alliance, the Warsaw Pact.

Lesson Vocabulary

charter a document from a group or organization that gives rights to people or groups

Lesson Summary
KOREA AND OTHER POSTWAR CONFLICTS

MODIFIED CORNELL NOTES

After World War II, the Korean peninsula in northeast Asia was divided into two zones: communist North Korea and non-communist South Korea. North Korea invaded South Korea in 1950. The United Nations, an international peacekeeping organization started after World War II, sent armed forces to stop the invasion. Americans led and made up most of these forces.

American forces under General Douglas MacArthur successfully drove North Korean forces back, then continued to push into North Korea. This action angered China, North Korea's ally, and the Chinese joined the war. President Truman wanted to avoid another world war. He called for peace agreements. Finally, after a truce was signed in 1953, Korea was divided at the 38th parallel into two countries, just as it had been before the war. A **demilitarized zone**—an area with no military forces—was set up on both sides of the border. To help preserve the truce, the United States continues to station thousands of American troops in South Korea. Although North and South Korea remained divided, this war showed that the United States and its allies would fight to stop Communist expansion.

By the 1950s, the United States and the Soviet Union had begun an arms race. As the Cold War continued, both sides built stockpiles of nuclear bombs and other weapons. Both the United States and Soviet Union competed with one another to gain influence in nations such as Somalia, Ethiopia, India, and Pakistan. In areas of Africa and Asia seeking to break free of European colonial control, local Communists, often backed by the Soviet Union, joined forces with other groups to fight in what Soviet leader Nikita Khrushchev called "wars of national liberation."

The Cold War also led to increased tensions in the United States. In 1950, State Department official Alger Hiss was convicted of **perjury**, or lying under oath. He had lied about his involvement in a Soviet spy ring within the United States. The United States government also learned that Julius and Ethel Rosenberg had passed atomic secrets to the Soviet Union, for which they were sentenced to death. From 1950 to 1954, Senator Joseph McCarthy led an effort to search for Communist spies within the American government. His reckless methods of public interrogation and accusations of disloyalty became known as McCarthyism, for which the U.S. Senate **censured**, or officially condemned, him. This ruined his political career.

Lesson Vocabulary

demilitarized zone an area in which military forces are prohibited

perjury lying under oath

censure to officially condemn

Name_____ Class_____ Date_____

MODIFIED CORNELL NOTES

After World War II, the United States faced the challenge of returning to peacetime conditions. Many feared that there would be no jobs for returning soldiers. Congress passed the GI Bill of Rights to help returning soldiers set up businesses, go to college, and build homes. President Truman tried to extend his Fair Deal, which encompassed reforms that extended liberal policies such as higher minimum wage and expanded Social Security, but conservatives in Congress blocked most of his plans. A Republican president, General Dwight Eisenhower, was elected in 1952. Eisenhower tried to follow a moderate course. He believed that the federal government should limit its spending, but he agreed to expand the benefits of Social Security.

The 1950s marked a period of prosperity in the United States. One reason for growth of the economy was the **baby boom** that occurred after World War II. Growing families needed new homes. Factories increased production of building materials, furniture, and other goods. More jobs were created, and businesses increased their **productivity**. Government projects, including Cold War military production, also contributed to economic growth. The economic good times led to a higher **standard of living** for Americans.

As the economy grew, American lifestyles changed. More Americans began to live in **suburbs**, or communities outside of cities. As suburbs grew, more people needed cars. Highways were built to link the nation. As a result of these factors, migration to the Sunbelt—the region stretching across the southern rim of the country—increased. In cultural life, television brought great change. News and entertainment were brought right into people's homes. Many television programs presented a singular view of an ideal middle-class family. Rock-and-roll became popular, particularly among teenagers, because it provided an opportunity for them to show their independence. Some writers, known as **beatniks**, strongly criticized what they saw as the growing materialism of American society and its lack of individuality.

Lesson Vocabulary

baby boom a large increase in birthrate from the late 1940s through the early 1960s

productivity the average output per worker

standard of living a measurement that determines how well people live based on the amount of goods, services, and leisure time people have

suburb a residential area on the outskirts of a city

beatnik a 1950s person who criticized American culture for conformity and devotion to business

MODIFIED CORNELL NOTES

In the 1950s, African Americans and other minorities continued to face discrimination. In the South, laws enforced the segregation of races. All across the country, African Americans could not get well-paying jobs. Many were kept from living and going to school where they pleased. Latinos faced similar problems. The civil rights movement to win civil rights for all Americans gathered strength. In 1948, President Truman ordered integration in the armed forces. When American troops were sent to fight in the Korean War, black and white soldiers fought together in the same units. Meanwhile, civil rights lawyers used the courts to win equal rights. In 1954, the Supreme Court ruled that segregation in schools was unconstitutional in the case *Brown v. Board of Education of Topeka*. When officials in Little Rock, Arkansas, refused to integrate the schools, President Eisenhower sent troops to enforce the court decision.

Dr. Martin Luther King, Jr., emerged as a leader in the civil rights movement. King believed in nonviolent civil disobedience, the refusal to obey unjust laws using nonviolent means. He led peaceful marches and organized boycotts against companies that practiced discrimination. King led a year-long boycott of a bus company in Montgomery, Alabama, in 1956. The company agreed to integrate the buses and to hire African American drivers. Despite these victories, segregation and discrimination remained widespread in the United States. However, by the 1960s, Congress passed civil rights laws. The Civil Rights Act of 1964 outlawed job discrimination. The Voting Rights Act of 1965 guaranteed that all citizens could vote.

During the 1970s, African Americans made some gains. African Americans were elected to government positions. Affirmative-action programs provided more job and educational opportunities for people who had faced discrimination in the past.

(Continues on the next page.)

Lesson Vocabulary

segregation the legal separation of people based on racial, ethnic, or other differences

civil rights movement the efforts of African Americans to win equal rights, particularly in the 1950s and 1960s

integration the mixing of different racial or ethnic groups

boycott to refuse to buy or use certain goods or services

affirmative-action a program to provide more job and education opportunities for people who faced discrimination in the past

Name_____ Class_____ Date_____

TOPIC
15
LESSON 4
Lesson Summary
CIVIL RIGHTS

(Continued from page 188)

Other minority groups fought for equal rights. Latinos worked to support the passage of the Voting Rights Act of 1975, which provided **bilingual** elections. Mexican Americans formed a union to protect **migrant workers**. Native Americans fought for their rights as well. The American Indian Movement (AIM) occupied Wounded Knee, South Dakota, to protest unfair treatment.

Women also struggled to win equal rights. In 1966, the National Organization for Women (NOW) was founded to work for equality in jobs, pay, and education. Gays and lesbians also struggled to win equal rights. Even though homosexuality was against the law in many places, gay rights activists drew attention to their cause during the 1960s by staging public protests in cities such as Washington D.C., New York City, and San Francisco.

Lesson Vocabulary
bilingual in two languages

migrant workers a person who moves from one region to another in search of work

TOPIC 15 LESSON 5
Lesson Summary
KENNEDY, JOHNSON, AND VIETNAM

MODIFIED CORNELL NOTES

The 1960s and 1970s were years of crisis and change for Americans and their leaders. In 1961, President John F. Kennedy took office. He hoped to use the government to help the economy and to help poor Americans.

Many regions around the world became battlegrounds in the Cold War struggle between the **superpowers**. Cuba was one of those battlegrounds. In the 1960s, the superpowers clashed over Cuba in the Bay of Pigs invasion and the Cuban missile crisis. In 1961, the United States led an attempt to overthrow the recently established communist government under Fidel Castro. About 1,400 Cuban **exiles**—people who have been forced to leave their own country—landed at the Bay of Pigs, but the invasion failed. The following year, the Soviet Union began to build a nuclear missile base on Cuba. President Kennedy responded forcefully. The U.S. Navy prevented the Soviets from shipping more missiles into Cuba. After a tense week, the Soviets agreed to remove the missiles. This was the closest that the United States and the Soviet Union ever came to a nuclear war.

Kennedy tried to contain the spread of communism in the world by promoting economic and scientific development. By giving aid to Latin American countries, Kennedy hoped to prevent the rise of communism, which many Latin Americans saw as a solution to chronic poverty. In 1961, Kennedy created an aid program known as the Alliance for Progress, which contributed aid to support education, healthcare, agriculture, and public services. He also set up the Peace Corps, which sent American volunteers to work in developing countries as teachers, engineers, and technical advisers. Through the Organization of American States, the United States promoted the development of transportation and industry in the Americas. After the Soviets had successfully launched the first satellite, *Sputnik I*, in 1957, Kennedy set up the National Aeronautics and Space Administration (NASA).

President Kennedy's term ended tragically in November 1963, when he was shot and killed. Vice President Lyndon Johnson took office. Johnson proposed the Great Society, his plan to improve the standard of living of every American. Congress created Medicare, which helped people over age 65 pay their medical bills.

(Continues on the next page.)

Lesson Vocabulary

superpower a nation with the military, political, and economic strength to influence events worldwide

exile a person who has been forced to leave his or her own country

TOPIC
15
LESSON 5

Lesson Summary
KENNEDY, JOHNSON, AND VIETNAM

(Continued from page 190)

After World War II, the French colony of Vietnam in Southeast Asia was divided into two nations. North Vietnam received aid from the Soviet Union. South Vietnam was backed by the United States. In the early 1960s, communist rebels in South Vietnam threatened to overthrow the government. President Kennedy believed in the **domino theory**. He reasoned that if South Vietnam fell to the communists, neighboring countries in Southeast Asia would also fall—like a row of dominoes. Kennedy sent military advisers to South Vietnam. Following the Gulf of Tonkin Resolution—allowing the President to take all necessary measures to repel any armed attack or prevent further aggression—the war in Vietnam **escalated**. President Johnson rapidly expanded the number of active troops in Vietnam. By 1968, more than 500,000 American troops had been sent to fight in the Vietnam War.

As the war became more intense, Americans divided into hawks and doves. Hawks felt that the United States had to stop the spread of communism. Doves said that the country should not interfere in a civil war among the Vietnamese. Also, they believed that the money spent on the war would be better spent at home. By the late 1960s, many antiwar protests took place, especially on college campuses. Many opposed the **draft**, or system of mandatory enlistment into the armed forces.

The United States tried to remove itself from the conflict. The turning point was the Tet Offensive. Communist rebels, known as the Vietcong, stormed Saigon, the capital of South Vietnam. It was clear that American troops could not win the war. Many Americans began to wonder how far the country should go in the fight against communism. Protest movements grew in the 1960s despite social reform. Young people joined the **counterculture movement**. They criticized competition and the drive for personal success, which they saw as characteristics of American society. They also protested the Vietnam War and called for peace and social equality.

Lesson Vocabulary

domino theory the belief that if South Vietnam fell to communism, other countries in the region would follow like a row of falling dominoes

escalate to expand

draft a law that requires people of a certain age to perform military service

counterculture movement a protest movement in the 1960s that rejected traditional American values and culture

Name_____ Class_____ Date_____

Lesson Summary
THE NIXON YEARS

MODIFIED CORNELL NOTES

Unease about the protests against the Vietnam War helped a Republican, Richard M. Nixon, win election as president in 1968. He claimed he wanted to help the **silent majority**, those who were disturbed by the unrest of the 1960s but did not protest publicly. Nixon faced a number of economic problems, such as **stagflation**, a combination of rising prices, high unemployment, and slow economic growth.

Nixon also had to decide how to deal with the war in Vietnam. Although initially sending more troops and authorizing additional bombings, Nixon pulled all American troops from Vietnam by 1974. Despite over a decade of American involvement in the region, the communist Khmer Rouge regime—which imposed a reign of terror on its own citizens—came to power in Cambodia, and North Vietnamese forces united Vietnam under one communist government.

Although unable to prevent the spread of communism in Cambodia and Vietnam, President Nixon looked for ways to ease world tensions. He improved relations with the communist People's Republic of China by visiting the country in 1972. Nixon toured the Great Wall of China and attended state dinners with Chinese leaders. This paved the way for formal diplomatic relations between the United States and China in 1979.

President Nixon also sought friendlier ties with the Soviet Union. He visited the country in 1972 in an effort to promote friendlier relations and reduce tensions between the two superpowers. The policy was known as **détente**. It resulted in increased trade and other contacts. More importantly, the two countries signed the SALT Agreement to limit nuclear weapons. Relations continued with the next two Presidents.

During his second term of office, Nixon faced the Watergate affair. He was accused of sending burglars into the Democratic Party headquarters in 1972. Nixon denied knowing about the burglary, but tapes he kept showed that he had tried to cover up the crime. He resigned in August 1974. Vice President Gerald Ford took office. Ford pardoned Nixon for the Watergate **scandal**.

Lesson Vocabulary

silent majority Americans who were disturbed by unrest in the 1960s but did not protest publicly

stagflation an economic situation that arises from a combination of rising prices, high unemployment, and slow economic growth

détente a policy that promotes the ending of strained or hostile tensions between countries

scandal an event that shocks people

TOPIC 15 Review Questions
POSTWAR AMERICA

Answer the questions below using the information in the Lesson Summaries on the previous pages.

Lesson 1: The Beginning of the Cold War

1. What were the purposes of the Truman Doctrine and the Marshall Plan?

_____

_____

2. Categorize What international organizations did the United States join in the postwar years in order to maintain the peace?

_____

_____

Lesson 2: Korea and Other Postwar Conflicts

3. What were the results of the Korean War?

_____

_____

4. Identify Main Ideas and Details Why was Senator Joseph McCarthy censured by the U.S. Senate?

_____

_____

Lesson 3: Eisenhower and Postwar America

5. Understand Causes What were some of the causes of the prosperity that the United States experienced in the 1950s?

_____

_____

6. What did the beatniks believe was wrong with American lifestyles in the 1950s?

_____

_____

Lesson 4: Civil Rights

7. How did the Supreme Court help to end segregation?

_____

_____

8. Identify Main Ideas How did Dr. Martin Luther King, Jr., put his the philosophy of nonviolence to battle against discrimination?

_____

_____

Lesson 5: Kennedy, Johnson, and Vietnam

9. Summarize What was the Bay of Pigs invasion?

_____

_____

10. Identify Main Ideas What was the Great Society, and what was one major part of it?

_____

_____

Lesson 6: The Nixon Years

11. What were the results of the Vietnam War?

_____

_____

12. Identify Main Ideas What led President Richard Nixon to resign from office?

_____

_____

TOPIC 16

Note Taking Study Guide
A GLOBAL SUPERPOWER FACING CHANGE

Focus Question: What were the foreign policy challenges that the United States faced in the 1980s and 1990s, and what were their results?

As you read, focus upon the challenges that the United States faced around the world from the 1970s through the 1990s. Think about what those challenges were and how the United States attempted to respond to them. Record your ideas.

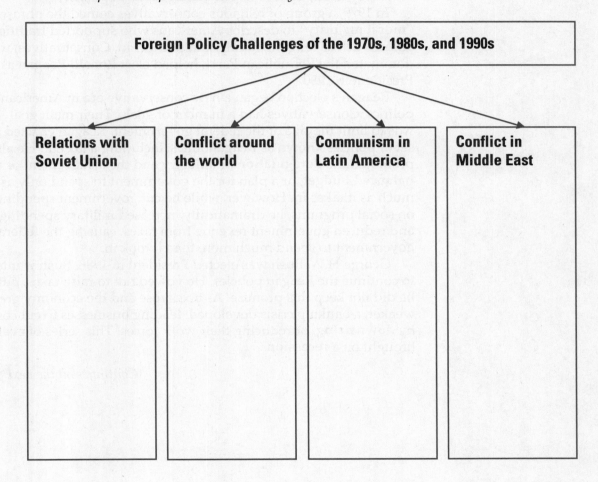

Foreign Policy Challenges of the 1970s, 1980s, and 1990s

Relations with Soviet Union	Conflict around the world	Communism in Latin America	Conflict in Middle East

TOPIC 16 LESSON 1

Lesson Summary
THE CONSERVATIVE REVOLUTION

MODIFIED CORNELL NOTES

Jimmy Carter became President in 1977, promising to bring new ideas to government. However, he was unable to bring down the high **inflation** that made life difficult for many Americans. In foreign policy, Carter took a firm stand on the need to support human rights around the world. He also was faced with the Iran hostage crisis and an energy crisis, both of which damaged his popularity.

In 1979, a group of religious conservatives coined the phrase "**moral majority**" to describe Americans who supported traditional values such as religion, family, and patriotism. Conservatives, who dominated the Republican Party, helped elect Ronald Reagan as President in 1980.

Reagan's election began a new conservative era in American politics. Conservatives had a number of goals. Their main goal was to limit the size of the federal government. Reagan enacted a set of policies known as Reaganomics, including a tax cut. He also promoted the **deregulation** of industry and the achievement of a **balanced budget**, or a plan for the government to spend only as much as it takes in. However, while he cut government spending on social programs, he dramatically increased military spending and reduced government revenue from taxes, causing the federal government to spend much more than it took in.

George H.W. Bush was elected President in 1988. Bush wanted to continue the Reagan policies. He vowed not to raise taxes, but he did not keep this promise. As taxes rose and the economy grew weaker, a banking crisis developed, leading businesses to cut costs by **downsizing**, or reducing their work forces. This series of events brought on a **recession**.

(Continues on the next page.)

Lesson Vocabulary

inflation a state in which prices keep rising

moral majority a religious organization that backed conservative political causes in the 1980s

deregulation a reduction of restrictions on businesses

balanced budget a condition that exists when the government spends only as much as it takes in

downsizing reducing a workforce

recession an economic slump that is milder than a depression

TOPIC 16 LESSON 1
Lesson Summary
THE CONSERVATIVE REVOLUTION

(Continued from page 196)

Bush also signed the North American Free Trade Agreement (NAFTA) in 1992. The purpose of this treaty was to end trade restrictions between Canada, Mexico, and the United States. Critics of NAFTA argued that free trade would cause a loss of American jobs. Companies might move factories to Mexico, where workers receive lower pay.

Democrat Bill Clinton won election as President in 1992. He supported NAFTA only after it was amended to include protections for labor and the environment. Congress approved NAFTA with these changes in 1993. After the agreement went into effect on January 1, 1994, trade between the three North American countries increased rapidly. The economy boomed. However, a Clinton plan to reform the healthcare system was defeated in Congress.

In 1994, Republicans won control of both houses of Congress. After many conflicts, Congress and Clinton compromised on several issues, including welfare reform. Clinton easily won re-election in 1996. His policies and the booming economy led to a federal budget **surplus** by 1998, or a situation in which the government takes in more than it spends.

Lesson Vocabulary
surplus extra; condition that exists when income exceeds spending

TOPIC 16 LESSON 2

Lesson Summary

THE END OF THE COLD WAR

The U.S. foreign policy of détente came to an abrupt end in 1979 after Soviet troops invaded Afghanistan. President Carter withdrew the SALT II Treaty from Congress. President Reagan then persuaded Congress to increase military spending for programs like Star Wars, which was designed to increase the United States' ability to destroy Soviet missiles from space. Distrust and tension between the two superpowers increased. When Poland's communist government imposed **martial law** to crack down on Solidarity, an independent labor union, the United States put economic pressure on Poland to end military rule.

Cracks began to appear in the Soviet empire in the mid-1980s. A new Soviet leader, Mikhail Gorbachev, started economic and political reforms. Gorbachev called for **glasnost**, a policy of openly discussing political and economic problems. Reagan and Gorbachev also held a series of **summit meetings**, or conferences between the highest-ranking officials of different nations. In 1987, the two leaders signed an arms control pact. As a result of glasnost, people were soon demanding change throughout the Soviet Union and the satellite states of Eastern Europe. By 1989, communist governments had fallen in most Eastern European countries.

In 1991, the Soviet Union ceased to exist. It broke up into 15 separate nations. The largest and most powerful of these was Russia. Some of the new countries began the difficult task of introducing democracy and free market economies. The United States and its Western allies attempted to help the transition by providing advice and economic aid. Finally, the long Cold War, which had cost the United States trillions of dollars and often divided the nation, came to an end.

The Cold War cost the United States over $6 trillion from 1946 to 1990, and countless lives. It also had divided Americans. However, after decades of fearing another world war, many Americans had the sense that the United States was free at last from serious external threats.

Lesson Vocabulary

martial law rule by the military instead of an elected government

glasnost a policy in the Soviet Union in the late 1980s of speaking openly about problems

summit meeting a conference between the highest-ranking officials of different nations

TOPIC 16 LESSON 3

Lesson Summary
REGIONAL CONFLICTS

In the post-Cold War world, the United States increased its role in world affairs as the only remaining superpower. It signed the Strategic Arms Reduction Treaty with the Soviet Union in 1991, which was honored by Russia and reduced both countries' nuclear arsenals. Sometimes it acted as a **mediator**, working to help conflicting parties iron out their differences.

American leaders continued to use military and diplomatic power where they thought it necessary. For example, the United States issued **sanctions** against South Africa to try to force an end to **apartheid**, a policy of strict racial segregation and discrimination.

During the 1990s, conflict erupted in the Eastern European country of Yugoslavia. After the fall of communism, Yugoslavia split into several different warring countries and many quarreling ethnic groups. In 1995, American negotiators helped arrange a peace treaty in Bosnia, one of the new countries. American troops went to Bosnia to help maintain the peace. America also offered to help Russia transition to a free-market economy and supported Russian President Boris Yeltsin's efforts at democratic reforms.

During the Cold War, the United States followed a policy of interventionism in Latin America. It intervened throughout the region where it saw a threat of communism. Between 1950 and 1990, American forces were sent to a number of Latin American countries. In the 1980s, the United States provided military aid to anticommunist groups in El Salvador and Nicaragua. The United States also sought to improve conditions in Latin America.

The United States also intervened in the affairs of some African and European nations. For example, in 1992 American forces led a United Nations mission to Somalia to keep the peace between opposing sides and help distribute food during a severe famine. American troops died while trying to restore order in the capital, leading to the government's decision to withdraw from the mission. The United States also helped arrange a peace agreement in Northern Ireland, a region that had experienced violent conflict between Catholics and Protestants for many years.

(Continues on the next page.)

Lesson Vocabulary

mediator an agent who helps conflicting parties iron out their differences

sanction a restriction on trade and finance designed to make a country change its policy

apartheid a strict separation of races practiced in South Africa

| TOPIC 16 LESSON 3 | **Lesson Summary** |
| | REGIONAL CONFLICTS |

MODIFIED CORNELL NOTES

(Continued from page 199)

The United States has had a long history of involvement in the Middle East. During this period it strongly supported Israel. Sometimes, this support led to reprisals from Middle Eastern nations. For example, after the United States sent aid to Israel in its 1973 war, Arab members of OPEC, the Organization of Petroleum Exporting Countries, retaliated by cutting off oil shipments to the United States. Other times, the United States was able to broker peace agreements between Israel and its Arab neighbors. Beginning in 1978, the United States hosted a series of meetings that led to the 1979 Camp David Accords, a peace treaty between Israel and Egypt in which Israel returned the Sinai Peninsula to Egypt in exchange for political recognition. The United States also led efforts to promote peace between Israelis and Palestinians by helping bring the Palestine Liberation Organization (PLO) and Israeli government to the bargaining table. The United States also led other nations in a successful effort to drive Iraq's forces from Kuwait in 1990, after Iraq had invaded its neighbor.

TOPIC 16 — Review Questions
A GLOBAL SUPERPOWER FACING CHANGE

Answer the questions below using the information in the Lesson Summaries on the previous pages.

Lesson 1: The Conservative Revolution

1. **Identify Main Ideas** What was the main goal of conservatives once Ronald Reagan was elected president?

   _____

   _____

2. What changes to the NAFTA treaty did President Bill Clinton want before supporting it?

   _____

   _____

Lesson 2: The End of the Cold War

3. **Sequence** Trace the development of nuclear arms control during the Carter and Reagan presidencies.

   _____

   _____

4. How did glasnost lead to the end of the Soviet Union?

   _____

   _____

Lesson 3: Regional Conflicts

5. **Identifying Supporting Details** What were three instances in the post–Cold War era in which the United States acted as a mediator?

   _____

   _____

6. How did some Middle Eastern countries react to U.S. support for Israel during its 1973 war?

   _____

   _____

TOPIC 17 — Note Taking Study Guide
MEETING NEW CHALLENGES

Focus Question: What challenges around the world and at home has the United States faced in recent decades? What has it done to address these challenges?

As you read, focus upon the new challenges that the United States has faced in recent decades both around the world and at home. Identify the problems that have arisen and what Americans have done to address them. Record both the challenges and responses.

Challenges	U.S. Response

TOPIC 17 LESSON 1

Lesson Summary
RESPONDING TO TERRORISM

The United States was shocked by terrorist attacks on September 11, 2001. Thousands of people were killed when airplanes struck the World Trade Center in New York City and the Pentagon near Washington, D.C. The United States reacted by launching a war on **terrorism** and countries that helped terrorists, such as Afghanistan. American and British troops were sent to fight in Afghanistan, in southwest Asia. A majority of Americans supported this effort.

The group that carried out the attacks was Al Qaeda, a jihadist **Islamic fundamentalist** group founded in 1988 by Osama bin Laden. Islamic fundamentalists believe that society should be governed according to a strict interpretation of Islamic scriptures and religious law. **Jihadism** is an Islamic fundamentalist movement that supports violence as a means to fight against those seen as enemies of Islam.

In 2002, President Bush accused Iraq of possessing **weapons of mass destruction (WMDs)**—chemical, biological, or nuclear weapons. The Iraq War began in March 2003 when American and British forces began bombing targets inside the country. An **insurgency**, or armed rebellion, arose against American forces and the new Iraqi government they had set up. Ethnic and religious violence was widespread. This violence was reduced temporarily with a surge of U.S. troops in 2007, but after Iraqis demanded withdrawal, U.S. troops finally left in 2013. By 2014, an Islamic fundamentalist group called the Islamic State had taken over much of western Iraq.

The United States faced ongoing challenges with regard to the jihadist movement. Despite U.S. attacks, jihadists took root in nations such as Yemen, Pakistan, and Somalia. Meanwhile, they fought for control in Iraq following U.S. withdrawal, and launched violent attacks in Algeria, Mali, and Nigeria. The U.S. government struggled to find an effective way to counter them.

Lesson Vocabulary

terrorism the use of violence and cruelty to achieve political goals

Islamic fundamentalist a Muslim who believes that Islamic religious texts should be taken literally

jihadism an Islamic fundamentalist movement that supports violence in the struggle against perceived enemies of Islam

weapons of mass destruction a chemical, biological, or nuclear weapon

insurgency an armed rebellion

TOPIC 17 LESSON 2

Lesson Summary
GLOBAL CHALLENGES

MODIFIED CORNELL NOTES

One goal of U.S. foreign policy was halting the spread of nuclear arms, or **nuclear proliferation**. The United States and many other countries signed the Nuclear Non-Proliferation Treaty (NPT), which committed nuclear powers such as the United States to reduce their stockpiles of nuclear weapons and prohibited countries that did not have them from acquiring them. Some countries, however, refused to sign the treaty. North Korea signed the treaty in 1985, but it continued to pursue its nuclear program, eventually leading to its withdrawal from the NPT in 2003. In 2006, it tested its first nuclear weapon. Despite being an NPT signatory, Iran was believed to have a nuclear weapons program. Negotiations between the United States and Iran to prevent it from developing nuclear weapons were opened in 2013.

In North Africa and Southwest Asia, the United States tried to resolve conflicts and committed itself to supporting democracy throughout the region. When the Arab Spring—a series of protests against undemocratic Arab governments—began in 2010, the United States openly supported the establishment of new, more democratic governments.

The United States also offered to assist its allies and other nations throughout the world in order to promote stability and democracy. Through the North Atlantic Treaty Organization, or NATO, it sought to protect ships in waters off the coast of Somalia from pirates. It also placed **sanctions** on Russia following the Russian invasion of Ukraine in early 2014. Furthermore, to counter threats posed by China to its neighbors, President Barack Obama announced a "pivot to Asia," which aims to strengthen economic and diplomatic relationships with nations in the Pacific Rim.

Lesson Vocabulary

nuclear proliferation the spread of nuclear weapons

sanction a restriction on trade and finance designed to make a country change its policies

Lesson Summary
A GLOBAL ECONOMY

In the 1990s and early 2000s, America's trade with other countries grew dramatically. In 1995, the United States joined the World Trade Organization. Other areas of the world also strengthened economic ties between nations. For example, the European Union was established, which created a more unified European market and attracted American investment. However, increasing globalization, or the spread of a global economy, posed potential problems. Some workers suffered when companies moved jobs overseas, and economic crises could spread more easily from one country to another.

After a recession in 2001, the Federal Reserve System lowered interest rates. This made it easier for home buyers to afford larger mortgages. As a result of the housing boom that followed, subprime mortgages—home loans to individuals with poor credit—increased. When home prices began to drop and interest rates increased, many people could no longer afford their homes. This led to a stock market and housing market crash in 2007, which had global effects. Trade slowed with partners such as Mexico and China, and Europe entered a recession. In response, Congress authorized a bailout of large banks and financial firms in 2008.

The next year, President Obama signed the American Recovery and Reinvestment Act into law. This law aimed to stimulate the economy and reduce unemployment. Still, by 2011, the unemployment rate remained high (around nine percent) and the housing market had not yet recovered. Tax cuts, wars, and slow economic growth had pushed America's debt level to its limit. President Obama asked Congress to raise the debt ceiling in 2011 and 2013. If the debt ceiling was not raised, America risked default, which would have caused the country to be unable to repay its debts.

Lesson Vocabulary

globalization the spread of links among the world's economies so that they form a global economy

mortgage a loan to purchase a piece of property that allows the lender to claim the property if the mortgage is not paid

subprime mortgage a type of mortgage granted to individuals with poor credit histories

debt ceiling a limit placed by law on the amount of money that the U.S. government can borrow

default a failure to repay a debt

TOPIC 17 LESSON 4

Lesson Summary
ADVANCES IN SCIENCE AND TECHNOLOGY

In the early 2000s, there were a number of new scientific and technological discoveries. NASA explored the solar system, giving special attention to the exploration of Mars. It also explored beyond the solar system, searching for new planets. In 1990, scientists began a project that led to the mapping of the human genome—the complete set of human **genes**, or the material that transfers inherited physical traits from parents to children. Other discoveries have been made in the field of **biotechnology**, which involves technology based on biology. These have helped to feed, fuel, and heal the world. For example, farmers have used biotechnology to increase crop production, while researchers have used it to make drugs to treat diseases.

The growth of the global economy during the late twentieth and early twenty-first centuries led to increased demand for **fossil fuels** such as coal, oil, and natural gas. Many people became increasingly concerned about the effects of **pollution**. In 1970, President Nixon created the Environmental Protection Agency, which later worked to reduce **emissions** of **greenhouse gases**, or gases that trap heat from the sun, causing Earth's temperature to increase.

Technology tied the world closer together even as it changed the way people did business. In the early 2000s, computers had a growing impact on people's lives. Using pagers, cell phones, personal computers, and the Internet, people around the world could exchange information instantly. E-commerce allowed businesses to trade online. Many Americans owned **smart phones**. These devices had the ability to connect to the Internet via radio signals. Tablet computers also became common.

Lesson Vocabulary

gene a bundle of hereditary material in organisms considered a building block of life

biotechnology technology based on biology

fossil fuel a fuel formed in the distant past that has limited supplies and cannot be renewed, such as oil, coal, and natural gas

pollution harmful impurities added to the environment

emission gas released into the air

greenhouse gas a gas, such as carbon dioxide, that blankets Earth and traps energy, causing the temperature to increase

smart phone a phone with sophisticated computing capability and an ability to connect to the Internet via radio signals

In the 2000 election, Vice President Al Gore ran against George W. Bush, son of former President George H.W. Bush. Gore won the popular vote by a narrow margin but lost the electoral vote. A number of votes in Florida were questioned, however. Gore called for a recount, but Bush opposed it. Both sides went to court. After 46 days, the Supreme Court ruled against Gore. As a result, Bush won the vote in the Electoral College. His election sharply divided the country.

The following year, the dot-com **bubble** burst, sending America into a recession. A bubble is a rise in prices based on expectations of future price rises, in this case affecting technology stocks on the stock market. In response to the recession, President Bush persuaded Congress to pass large tax cuts to stimulate the economy. The attacks on September 11, 2001, however, led the United States to spend additional funds on a war on terrorism. The federal **deficit**—or the amount by which its spending was greater than its income—increased.

Democratic Senator Barack Obama of Illinois won the 2008 presidential election. Many Americans opposed the wars in Iraq and Afghanistan and struggled with the deepening economic crisis that followed the collapse of a housing bubble. Obama allowed some of the Bush tax cuts to expire and withdrew U.S. troops from Iraq in 2011. In general, Obama expanded the fight against terrorism. In addition to Afghanistan, American armed forces were involved in combat missions against terrorists in Yemen, Pakistan, and Somalia in 2012.

President Obama also worked to pass the Affordable Care Act, which required all Americans to purchase health insurance and provided funding to help lower-income Americans pay for it. Obama faced a divided Congress after 2010, when Republicans gained control of the House of Representatives. However, despite frequent political gridlock on issues ranging from healthcare to budgets, Obama won re-election to the presidency in 2012.

(Continues on the next page.)

Lesson Vocabulary

bubble a situation that occurs when buyers drive prices higher than the actual worth of the product or stock in the hope that prices will rise higher still

deficit an amount of spending greater than the amount of income

MODIFIED CORNELL NOTES

(Continued from page 207)

Throughout the 2000s, the United States saw increases in immigration, a changing ethnic makeup, and growing numbers of older Americans. Latinos outnumbered African Americans for the first time in 2010, while the elderly population of America was projected to rise from 13 percent of the total in 2014 to 20 percent by 2040.

The U.S. Supreme Court also heard cases involving **affirmative action**—preferences for hiring African Americans, women, or members of other groups discriminated against—and gay rights. In 2003 the court ruled that universities could not use rigid formulas to give preference to minority members over others, and in 2013 it ruled that same-sex married couples were entitled to federal benefits just like other married couples.

During these years, America underwent dramatic changes in its population and role in world affairs. Still, it maintained a strong sense of national pride, commitment to economic opportunity, and devotion to freedom.

Lesson Vocabulary

affirmative action an active effort to improve the employment or educational opportunities of members of minority groups and women

TOPIC 17

Review Questions

MEETING NEW CHALLENGES

Answer the questions below using the information in the Lesson Summaries on the previous pages.

Lesson 1: Responding to Terrorism

1. Who carried out the 2001 attacks against the World Trade Center in New York City and the Pentagon?

_____

_____

2. Sequence Events After President George W. Bush accused Iraq of possessing weapons of mass destruction, what series of events transpired?

_____

_____

Lesson 2: Global Challenges

3. Draw Conclusions Why do you think U.S. foreign policy has made nuclear nonproliferation one of its main goals?

_____

_____

4. What is the purpose of President Obama's "pivot to Asia" policy?

_____

_____

Lesson 3: A Global Economy

5. What three factors combined to push America's debt level to new limits in 2011 and 2013?

_____

_____

6. Identifying Supporting Details What are some of the downsides of globalization?

_____

_____

TOPIC 17

Review Questions (continued)

MEETING NEW CHALLENGES

Lesson 4: Advances in Science and Technology

7. **Make Inferences** How has the growth of the global economy caused environmental problems?

_____

_____

8. Name three examples of technology that changed the way people did business in the early 2000s.

_____

_____

Lesson 5: Domestic Challenges

9. What was President Barack Obama's approach to the war on terror?

_____

_____

10. **Summarize** How did the American population change in the 2000s?

_____

_____